AN ICELAND FISHERMAN

By

Pierre Loti

Translated by M. Jules Cambon

D1513265

PIERRE LOTI

PIERRE LOTI

The first appearance of Pierre Loti's works, twenty years ago, caused a sensation throughout those circles wherein the creations of intellect and imagination are felt, studied, and discussed. The author was one who, with a power which no one had wielded before him, carried off his readers into exotic lands, and whose art, in appearance most simple, proved a genuine enchantment for the imagination. It was the time when M. Zola and his school stood at the head of the literary movement. There breathed forth from Loti's writings an all-penetrating fragrance of poesy, which liberated French literary ideals from the heavy and oppressive yoke of the Naturalistic school. Truth now soared on unhampered pinions, and the reading world was completely won by the unsurpassed intensity and faithful accuracy with which he depicted the alluring charms of far-off scenes, and painted the naive soul of the races that seem to endure in the isles of the Pacific as surviving representatives of the world's infancy.

It was then learned that this independent writer was named in real life Louis Marie Julien Viaud, and that he was a naval officer. This very fact, that he was not a writer by profession, added indeed to his success. He actually had seen that which he was describing, he had lived that which he was relating. What in any other man would have seemed but research and oddity, remained natural in the case of a sailor who returned each year with a manuscript in his hand. Africa, Asia, the isles of the Pacific, were the usual scenes of his dramas. Finally from France itself, and from the oldest provinces of France, he drew subject-matter for two of his novels, *An Iceland Fisherman* and *Ramuntcho*. This proved a surprise. Our Breton sailors and our Basque mountaineers were not less foreign to the Parisian drawing-room than was Aziyade or the little Rahahu. One claimed to have a knowledge of Brittany, or of the Pyrenees, because one had visited Dinard or Biarritz; while in reality neither Tahiti nor the Isle of Paques could have remained more completely unknown to us.

The developments of human industry have brought the extremities of the world nearer together; but the soul of each race continues to cloak itself in its own individuality and to remain a mystery to the rest of the world. One trait alone is common to all: the infinite sadness of human destiny. This it was that Loti impressed so vividly on the reading world.

His success was great. Though a young man as yet, Loti saw his work crowned with what in France may be considered the supreme sanction: he was elected to membership in the French Academy. His name became coupled with those of Bernardin de St. Pierre and of Chateaubriand. With the sole exception of the author of *Paul and Virginia* and of the writer of *Atala*, he seemed to be one without predecessor and without a master. It may be well here to inquire how much reason there is for this assertion, and what novel features are presented in his work.

It has become a trite saying that French genius lacks the sense of Nature, that the French tongue is colourless, and therefore wants the most striking feature of poetry. If we abandoned for one moment the domain of letters and took a comprehensive view of the field of art, we might be permitted to express astonishment at the passing of so summary a judgment on the genius of a nation which has, in the real sense of the term, produced two such painters of Nature as Claude Lorrain and Corot. But even in the realm of letters it is easily seen that this mode of thinking is due largely to insufficient knowledge of the language's resources, and to a study of French literature which does not extend beyond the seventeenth century. Without going back to the Duke of Orleans and to Villon, one need only read a few of the poets of the sixteenth century to be struck by the prominence given to Nature in their writings. Nothing is more delightful than Ronsard's word-paintings of his sweet country of Vendome. Until the day of Malherbe, the didactic Regnier and the Calvinistic Marot are the only two who could be said to give colour to the preconceived and prevalent notion as to the dryness of French poetry. And even after Malherbe, in the seventeenth century, we find that La Fontaine, the most truly French of French writers, was a passionate lover of Nature. He who can see nothing in the latter's fables beyond the little dramas which they unfold and the ordinary moral which the poet draws therefrom, must confess that he fails to understand him. His landscapes possess precision, accuracy, and life, while such is the fragrance of his speech that it seems laden with the fresh perfume of the fields and furrows.

Racine himself, the most penetrating and the most psychological of poets, is too well versed in the human soul not to have felt its intimate union with Nature. His magnificent verse in Phedre,

"Ah, que ne suis-je assise a l'ombre des forets!"

is but the cry of despair, the appeal, filled with anguish, of a heart that is troubled and which oft has sought peace and alleviation amid the cold indifference of inanimate things. The small place given to Nature in the French literature of the seventeenth century is not to be ascribed to the language nor explained by a lack of sensibility on the part of the race. The true cause is to be found in the spirit of that period; for investigation will disclose that the very same condition then characterized the literatures of England, of Spain, and of Italy.

We must bear in mind that, owing to an almost unique combination of circumstances, there never has been a period when man was more convinced of the nobility and, I dare say it, of the sovereignty of man, or was more inclined to look upon the latter as a being independent of the external world. He did not suspect the intimately close bonds which unite the creature to the medium in which it lives. A man of the world in the seventeenth century was utterly without a notion of those truths which in their ensemble constitute the natural sciences. He crossed the threshold of life possessed of a deep classical instruction, and all-imbued with stoical ideas of virtue. At the same time, he had received the mould of a strong but narrow Christian education, in which nothing figured save his relations with God. This twofold training elevated his soul and fortified his will, but wrenched him violently from all communion with Nature. This is the standpoint from which we must view the heroes of Corneille, if we would understand those extraordinary souls which, always at the highest degree of tension, deny themselves, as a weakness, everything that resembles tenderness or pity. Again, thus and thus alone can we explain how Descartes, and with him all the philosophers of his century, ran counter to all common sense, and refused to recognise that animals might possess a soul-like principle which, however remotely, might link them to the human being.

When, in the eighteenth century, minds became emancipated from the narrow restrictions of religious discipline, and when method was introduced into the study of scientific problems, Nature took her revenge as well in literature as in all other fields of human thought. Rousseau it was who inaugurated the movement in France, and the whole of Europe followed in the wake of France. It may even be declared that the reaction against the seventeenth century was in many respects excessive, for the eighteenth century gave itself up to a species of sentimental debauch. It is none the less a fact that the author of *La Nouvelle Heloise* was the first to blend the moral life of man with his exterior surroundings. He felt the savage beauty and grandeur of the mountains of Switzerland, the grace of the Savoy horizons, and the more familiar elegance of the Parisian suburbs. We may say that he opened the eye of humanity to the spectacle which the world offered it. In Germany, Lessing, Goethe, Hegel, Schelling have proclaimed him their master; while even in England, Byron, and George Eliot herself, have recognised all that they owed to him.

The first of Rosseau's disciples in France was Bernardin de St. Pierre, whose name has frequently been recalled in connection with Loti. Indeed, the charming masterpiece of *Paul and Virginia* was the first example of exoticism in literature; and thereby it excited the curiosity of our fathers at the same time that it dazzled them by the wealth and brilliancy of its descriptions.

Then came Chateaubriand; but Nature with him was not a mere background. He sought from it an accompaniment, in the musical sense of the term, to the movements of his soul; and being somewhat prone to melancholy, his taste seems to have favoured sombre landscapes, stormy and tragical. The entire romantic school was born from him, Victor Hugo and George Sand, Theophile Gautier who draws from the French tongue resources unequalled in wealth and colour, and even M. Zola himself, whose naturalism, after all, is but the last form and, as it were, the end of romanticism, since it would be difficult to discover in him any characteristic that did not exist, as a germ at least, in Balzac.

I have just said that Chateaubriand sought in Nature an accompaniment to the movements of his soul: this was the case with all the romanticists. We do not find Rene, Manfred, Indiana, living in the midst of a tranquil and monotonous Nature. The storms of heaven must respond to the storms of their soul; and it is a fact that all these great writers, Byron as well as Victor Hugo, have not so much contemplated and seen Nature as they have interpreted it through the medium of their own passions; and it is in this sense that the keen Amiel could justly remark that a landscape is a condition or a state of the soul.

M. Loti does not merely interpret a landscape; though perhaps, to begin with, he is unconscious of doing more. With him, the human being is a part of Nature, one of its very expressions, like animals and plants, mountain forms and sky tints. His characters are what they are only because they issue forth from the medium in which they live. They are truly creatures, and not gods inhabiting the earth. Hence their profound and striking reality.

Hence also one of the peculiar characteristics of Loti's workers. He loves to paint simple souls, hearts close to Nature, whose primitive passions are singularly similar to those of animals. He is happy in the isles of the Pacific or on the borders of Senegal; and when he shifts his scenes into old Europe it is never with men and women of the world that he entertains us.

What we call a man of the world is the same everywhere; he is moulded by the society of men, but Nature and the universe have no place in his life and thought. M. Paul Bourget's heroes might live without distinction in Newport or in Monte Carlo; they take root nowhere, but live in the large cities, in winter resorts and in drawing-rooms as transient visitors in temporary abiding-places.

Loti seeks his heroes and his heroines among those antique races of Europe which have survived all conquests, and which have preserved, with their native tongue, the individuality of their character. He met Ramuntcho in the Basque country, but dearer than all to him is Brittany: here it was that he met his Iceland fishermen.

The Breton soul bears an imprint of Armorica's primitive soil: it is melancholy and noble. There is an undefinable charm about those arid lands and those sod-flanked hills of granite, whose sole horizon is the far-stretching sea. Europe ends here, and beyond remains only the broad expanse of the ocean. The poor people who dwell here are silent and tenacious: their heart is full of tenderness and of dreams. Yann, the Iceland fisherman, and his sweetheart, Gaud of Paimpol, can only live here, in the small houses of Brittany, where people huddle together in a stand against the storms which come howling from the depths of the Atlantic.

Loti's novels are never complicated with a mass of incidents. The characters are of humble station and their life is as simple as their soul. *Aziyade, The Romance of a Spahi, An Iceland Fisherman, Ramuntcho*, all present the story of a love and a separation. A departure, or death itself, intervenes to put an end to the romance. But the cause matters little; the separation is the same; the hearts are broken; Nature survives; it covers over and absorbs the miserable ruins which we leave behind us. No one better than Loti has ever brought out the frailty of all things pertaining to us, for no one better than he has made us realize the persistency of life and the indifference of Nature.

This circumstance imparts to the reading of M. Loti's works a character of peculiar sadness. The trend of his novels is not one that incites curiosity; his heroes are simple, and the atmosphere in which they live is foreign to us. What saddens us is not their history, but the undefinable impression that our pleasures are nothing and that we are but an accident. This is a thought common to the degree of triteness among moralists and theologians; but as they present it, it fails to move us. It troubles us as presented by M. Loti, because he has known how to give it all the force of a sensation.

How has he accomplished this?

He writes with extreme simplicity, and is not averse to the use of vague and indefinite expressions. And yet the wealth and precision of Gautier's and Hugo's language fail to endow their landscapes with the striking charm and intense life which are to be found in those of Loti. I can find no other reason for this than that which I have suggested above: the landscape, in Hugo's and in Gautier's scenes, is a background and nothing more; while Loti makes it the predominating figure of his drama. Our sensibilities are necessarily aroused before this apparition of Nature, blind, inaccessible, and all-powerful as the Fates of old.

It may prove interesting to inquire how Loti contrived to sound such a new note in art.

He boasted, on the day of his reception into the French Academy, that he had never read. Many protested, some smiled, and a large number of persons refused to believe the assertion. Yet the statement was actually quite credible, for the foundation and basis of M. Loti rest on a naive simplicity which makes him very sensitive to the things of the outside world, and gives him a perfect comprehension of simple souls. He is not a reader, for he is not imbued with book notions of things; his ideas of them are direct, and everything with him is not memory, but reflected sensation.

On the other hand, that sailor-life which had enabled him to see the world, must have confirmed in him this mental attitude. The deck officer who watches the vessel's course may do nothing which could distract his attention; but while ever ready to act and always unoccupied, he thinks, he dreams, he listens to the voices of the sea; and everything about him is of interest to him, the shape of the clouds, the aspect of skies and waters. He knows that a mere board's thickness is all that separates him and defends him from death. Such is the habitual state of mind which M. Loti has brought to the colouring of his books.

He has related to us how, when still a little child, he first beheld the sea. He had escaped from the parental home, allured by the brisk and pungent air and by the "peculiar noise, at once feeble and great," which could be heard beyond little hills of sand to which led a certain path. He recognised the sea; "before me something appeared, something sombre and noisy, which had loomed up from all sides at once, and which seemed to have no end; a moving expanse which struck me with mortal vertigo; . . . above was stretched out full a sky all of one piece, of a dark gray colour like a heavy mantle; very, very far away, in unmeasurable depths of horizon, could be seen a break, an opening between sea and sky, a long empty crack, of a light pale yellow." He felt a sadness unspeakable, a sense of desolate solitude, of abandonment, of exile. He ran back in haste to unburden his soul upon his mother's bosom, and, as he says, "to seek consolation with her for a thousand anticipated, indescribable pangs, which had wrung my heart at the sight of that vast green, deep expanse."

A poet of the sea had been born, and his genius still bears a trace of the shudder of fear experienced that evening by Pierre Loti the little child.

Loti was born not far from the ocean, in Saintonge, of an old Huguenot family which had numbered many sailors among its members. While yet a mere child he thumbed the old Bible which formerly, in the days of persecution, had been read only with cautious secrecy; and he perused the vessel's ancient records wherein mariners long since gone had noted, almost a century before, that "the weather was good," that "the wind was favourable," and that "doradoes or gilt-heads were passing near the ship."

He was passionately fond of music. He had few comrades, and his imagination was of the exalted kind. His first ambition was to be a minister, then a missionary; and finally he decided to become a sailor. He wanted to see the world, he had the curiosity of things; he was inclined to search for the strange and the unknown; he must seek that sensation, delightful and fascinating to complex souls, of betaking himself off, of withdrawing from his own world, of breaking with his own mode of life, and of creating for himself voluntary regrets.

He felt in the presence of Nature a species of disquietude, and experienced therefrom sensations which might almost be expressed in colours: his head, he himself states, "might be compared to a camera, filled with sensitive plates." This power of vision permitted him to apprehend only the appearance of things, not their reality; he was conscious of the nothingness of nothing, of the dust of dust. The remnants of his religious education intensified still more this distaste for the external world.

He was wont to spend his summer vacation in the south of France, and he preserved its warm sunny impressions. It was only later that he became acquainted with Brittany. She inspired him at first with a feeling of oppression and of sadness, and it was long before he learned to love her.

Thus was formed and developed, far from literary circles and from Parisian coteries, one of the most original writers that had appeared for a long time. He noted his impressions while touring the world; one fine morning he published them, and from the very first the reading public was won. He related his adventures and his own romance. The question could then be raised whether his skill and art would prove as consummate if he should deviate from his own personality to write what might be termed impersonal poems; and it is precisely in this last direction that he subsequently produced what are now considered his masterpieces.

A strange writer assuredly is this, at once logical and illusive, who makes us feel at the same time the sensation of things and that of their nothingness. Amid so many works wherein the luxuries of the Orient, the quasi animal life of the Pacific, the burning passions of Africa, are painted with a vigour of imagination never witnessed before his advent, *An Iceland Fisherman* shines forth with incomparable brilliancy. Something of the pure soul of Brittany is to be found in these melancholy pages, which, so long as the French tongue endures, must evoke the admiration of artists, and must arouse the pity and stir the emotions of men.

JULES CAMBON. BIOGRAPHICAL NOTE

The real name of PIERRE LOTI is LOUIS MARIE JULIEN VIAUD. He was born of Protestant parents, in the old city of Rochefort, on the 14th of January, 1850. In one of his pleasant volumes of autobiography, "Le

Roman d'un Enfant," he has given a very pleasing account of his childhood, which was most tenderly cared for and surrounded with indulgences. At a very early age he began to develop that extreme sensitiveness to external influences which has distinguished him ever since. He was first taught at a school in Rochefort, but at the age of seventeen, being destined for the navy, he entered the great French naval school, Le Borda, and has gradually risen in his profession. His pseudonym is said to have had reference to his extreme shyness and reserve in early life, which made his comrades call him after "le Loti," an Indian flower which loves to blush unseen. He was never given to books or study (when he was received at the French Academy, he had the courage to say, "Loti ne sait pas lire"), and it was not until his thirtieth year that he was persuaded to write down and publish certain curious experiences at Constantinople, in "Aziyade," a book which, like so many of Loti's, seems half a romance, half an autobiography. He proceeded to the South Seas, and, on leaving Tahiti, published the Polynesian idyl, originally called "Raharu," which was reprinted as "Le Mariage de Loti" (1880), and which first introduced to the wider public an author of remarkable originality and charm. Loti now became extremely prolific, and in a succession of volumes chronicled old exotic memories or manipulated the journal of new travels. "Le Roman d'un Spahi," a record of the melancholy adventures of a soldier in Senegambia, belongs to 1881. In 1882 Loti issued a collection of short studies under the general title of "Fleurs d'Ennui." In 1883 he achieved the widest celebrity, for not only did he publish "Mon Frere Yves," a novel describing the life of a French bluejacket in all parts of the world—perhaps, on the whole, to this day his most characteristic production—but he was involved in a public discussion in a manner which did him great credit. While taking part as a naval officer in the Tonquin war, Loti had exposed in a Parisian newspaper a series of scandals which succeeded on the capture of Hue, and, being recalled, he was now suspended from the service for more than a year. He continued for some time nearly silent, but in 1886, he published a novel of life among the Breton fisher-folk, entitled "Pecheurs d'Islande"; this has been the most popular of all his writings. In 1887 he brought out a volume of extraordinary merit, which has never received the attention it deserves; this is "Propos d'Exil," a series of short studies of exotic places, in Loti's peculiar semi-autobiographic style. The fantastic romance of Japanese manners, "Madame Chrysantheme," belongs to the same year. Passing over one or two slighter productions, we come to 1890, to "Au Maroc," the record of a journey to Fez in company with a French embassy. A collection of strangely confidential and sentimental reminiscences, called "Le Livre de la Pitie et de la

Mort," belongs to 1891. Loti was on board his ship at the port of Algiers when news was brought to him of his election, on the 21st of May, 1891, to the French Academy. Since he has become an Immortal the literary activity of Pierre Loti has somewhat declined. In 1892 he published "Fantome d'Orient," another dreamy study of life in Constantinople, a sort of continuation of "Aziyade." He has described a visit to the Holy Land in three volumes, "Le Desert," "Jerusalem," "La Galilee" (1895-96), and he has written one novel, "Ramentcho" (1897), a story of manners in the Basque province, which is quite on a level with his best work. In 1898 he collected his later essays as "Figures et Choses qui passaient." In 1899-1900 Loti visited British India, and in the autumn of the latter year China; and he has described what he saw there, after the seige, in a charming volume, "Derniers Jours de Pekin," 1902.

E. G.

AN ICELAND FISHERMAN

by Pierre Loti

PART 1 — ON THE ICY SEA

CHAPTER I—THE FISHERMEN

There they were, five huge, square-built seamen, drinking away together in the dismal cabin, which reeked of fish-pickle and bilge-water. The overhead beams came down too low for their tall statures, and rounded off at one end so as to resemble a gull's breast, seen from within. The whole rolled gently with a monotonous wail, inclining one slowly to drowsiness.

Outside, beyond doubt, lay the sea and the night; but one could not be quite sure of that, for a single opening in the deck was closed by its weather-hatch, and the only light came from an old hanging-lamp, swinging to and fro. A fire shone in the stove, at which their saturated clothes were drying, and giving out steam that mingled with the smoke from their clay pipes.

Their massive table, fitted exactly to its shape, occupied the whole space; and there was just enough room for moving around and sitting upon the narrow lockers fastened to the sides. Thick beams ran above them, very nearly touching their heads, and behind them yawned the berths, apparently hollowed out of the solid timbers, like recesses of a vault wherein to place the dead. All the wainscoting was rough and worn, impregnated with damp and salt, defaced and polished by the continual rubbings of their hands.

They had been drinking wine and cider in their pannikins, and the sheer enjoyment of life lit up their frank, honest faces. Now, they lingered at table chatting, in Breton tongue, on women and marriage. A china statuette of the Virgin Mary was fastened on a bracket against the midship partition, in the place of honour. This patron saint of our sailors was rather antiquated, and painted with very simple art; yet these porcelain images live much longer than real men, and her red and blue robe still seemed very fresh in the midst of the sombre greys of the poor wooden box. She must have listened to many an ardent prayer in deadly hours; at her feet were nailed two nosegays of artificial flowers and a rosary.

These half-dozen men were dressed alike; a thick blue woollen jersey clung to the body, drawn in by the waist-belt; on the head was worn the waterproof helmet, known as the sou'-wester. These men were of different ages. The skipper might have been about forty; the three others between twenty-five and thirty. The youngest, whom they called Sylvestre or "Lurlu," was only seventeen, yet already a man for height and strength; a fine curly black beard covered his cheeks; still he had childlike eyes, bluish-grey in hue, and sweet and tender in expression.

Huddled against one another, for want of space, they seemed to feel downright comfort, snugly packed in their dark home.

Outside spread the ocean and night—the infinite solitude of dark fathomless waters. A brass watch, hung on the wall, pointed to eleven o'clock—doubtless eleven at night—and upon the deck pattered the drizzling rain.

Among themselves, they treated these questions of marriage very merrily; but without saying anything indecent. No, indeed, they only sketched plans for those who were still bachelors, or related funny stories happening at home at wedding-feasts. Sometimes with a happy laugh they made some rather too free remarks about the fun in love-making. But love-making, as these men understand it, is always a healthy sensation, and for all its coarseness remains tolerably chaste.

But Sylvestre was worried, because a mate called Jean (which Bretons pronounce "Yann") did not come down below. Where could Yann be, by the way? was he lashed to his work on deck? Why did he not come below to take his share in their feast?

"It's close on midnight, hows'ever," observed the captain; and drawing himself up he raised the scuttle with his head, so as to call Yann that way.

Then a weird glimmer fell from above.

"Yann! Yann! Look alive, matey!"

"Matey" answered roughly from outside while through the half-opened hatchway the faint light kept entering like that of dawn. Nearly midnight, yet it looked like a peep of day, or the light of the starry gloaming, sent from afar through mystic lenses of magicians.

When the aperture closed, night reigned again, save for the small lamp, "sended" now and again aside, which shed its yellow light. A man in clogs was heard coming down the wooden steps.

He entered bent in two like a big bear, for he was a giant. At first he made a wry face, holding his nose, because of the acrid smell of the souse.

He exceeded a little too much the ordinary proportions of man, especially in breadth, though he was straight as a poplar. When he faced you the muscles of his shoulders, moulded under his blue jersey, stood out like great globes at the tops of his arms. His large brown eyes were very mobile, with a grand, wild expression.

14

Sylvestre threw his arms round Yann, and drew him towards him tenderly, after the fashion of children. Sylvestre was betrothed to Yann's sister, and he treated him as an elder brother, of course. And Yann allowed himself to be pulled about like a young lion, answering by a kind smile that showed his white teeth. These were somewhat far apart, and appeared quite small. His fair moustache was rather short, although never cut. It was tightly curled in small rolls above his lips, which were most exquisitely and delicately modelled, and then frizzed off at the ends on either side of the deep corners of his mouth. The remainder of his beard was shaven, and his highly coloured cheeks retained a fresh bloom like that of fruit never yet handled.

When Yann was seated, the mugs were filled up anew.

The lighting of all the pipes was an excuse for the cabin boy to smoke a few wiffs himself. He was a robust little fellow, with round cheeks—a kind of little brother to them all, more or less related to one another as they were; otherwise his work had been hard enough for the darling of the crew. Yann let him drink out of his own glass before he was sent to bed. Thereupon the important topic of marriage was revived.

"But I say, Yann," asked Sylvestre, "when are we going to celebrate your wedding?"

"You ought to be ashamed," said the master; "a hulking chap like you, twenty-seven years old and not yet spliced; ho, ho! What must the lasses think of you when they see you roll by?"

Yann answered by snapping his thick fingers with a contemptuous look for the women folk. He had just worked off his five years' government naval service; and it was as master-gunner of the fleet that he had learned to speak good French and hold sceptical opinions. He hemmed and hawed and then rattled off his latest love adventure, which had lasted a fortnight.

It happened in Nantes, a Free-and-Easy singer for the heroine. One evening, returning from the waterside, being slightly tipsy, he had entered the music hall. At the door stood a woman selling big bouquets at twenty francs apiece. He had bought one without quite knowing what he should do with it, and before he was much more than in had thrown it with great force at the vocalist upon the stage, striking her full in the face, partly as a rough declaration of love, partly through disgust for the painted doll that was too pink for his taste. The blow had felled the woman to the boards, and—she worshipped him during the three following weeks.

"Why, bless ye, lads, when I left she made me this here present of a real gold watch."

The better to show it them he threw it upon the table like a worthless toy.

This was told with coarse words and oratorical flourishes of his own. Yet this commonplace of civilized life jarred sadly among such simple men, with the grand solemnity of the ocean around them; in the glimmering of midnight, falling from above, was an impression of the fleeting summers of the far north country.

These ways of Yann greatly pained and surprised Sylvestre. He was a girlish boy, brought up in respect for holy things, by an old grandmother, the widow of a fisherman in the village of Ploubazlanec. As a tiny child he used to go every day with her to kneel and tell his beads over his mother's grave. From the churchyard on the cliff the grey waters of the Channel, wherein his father had disappeared in a shipwreck, could be seen in the far distance.

As his grandmother and himself were poor he had to take to fishing in his early youth, and his childhood had been spent out on the open water. Every night he said his prayers, and his eyes still wore their religious purity. He was captivating though, and next to Yann the finest-built lad of the crew. His voice was very soft, and its boyish tones contrasted markedly with his tall height and black beard; as he had shot up very rapidly he was almost puzzled to find himself grown suddenly so tall and big. He expected to marry Yann's sister soon, but never yet had answered any girl's love advances.

There were only three sleeping bunks aboard, one being double-berthed, so they "turned in" alternately.

When they had finished their feast, celebrating the Assumption of their patron saint, it was a little past midnight. Three of them crept away to bed in the small dark recesses that resembled coffin-shelves; and the three others went up on deck to get on with their often interrupted, heavy labour of fish-catching; the latter were Yann, Sylvestre, and one of their fellow-villagers known as Guillaume.

It was daylight, the everlasting day of those regions—a pale, dim light, resembling no other—bathing all things, like the gleams of a setting sun. Around them stretched an immense colourless waste, and excepting the planks of their ship, all seemed transparent, ethereal, and fairy-like. The eye could not distinguish what the scene might be: first it appeared as a quivering mirror that had no objects to reflect; and in the distance it became a desert of vapour; and beyond that a void, having neither horizon nor limits.

The damp freshness of the air was more intensely penetrating than dry frost; and when breathing it, one tasted the flavour of brine. All was calm, and the rain had ceased; overhead the clouds, without form or colour, seemed to conceal that latent light that could not be explained; the eye could see clearly, yet one was still conscious of the night; this dimness was all of an indefinable hue.

The three men on deck had lived since their childhood upon the frigid seas, in the very midst of their mists, which are vague and troubled as the background of dreams. They were accustomed to see this varying infinitude play about their paltry ark of planks, and their eyes were as used to it as those of the great free ocean-birds.

The boat rolled gently with its everlasting wail, as monotonous as a Breton song moaned by a sleeper. Yann and Sylvestre had got their bait and lines ready, while their mate opened a barrel of salt, and whetting his long knife went and sat behind them, waiting.

He did not have long to wait, or they either. They scarcely had thrown their lines into the calm, cold water in fact, before they drew in huge heavy fish, of a steel-grey sheen. And time after time the codfish let themselves be hooked in a rapid and unceasing silent series. The third man ripped them open with his long knife, spread them flat, salted and counted them, and piled up the lot—which upon their return would constitute their fortune—behind them, all still redly streaming and still sweet and fresh.

The hours passed monotonously, while in the immeasurably empty regions beyond the light slowly changed till it grew less unreal. What at first had appeared a livid gloaming, like a northern summer's eve, became now, without any intervening "dark hour before dawn," something like a smiling morn, reflected by all the facets of the oceans in fading, roseate-edged streaks.

"You really ought to marry, Yann," said Sylvestre, suddenly and very seriously this time, still looking into the water. (He seemed to know somebody in Brittany, who had allowed herself to be captivated by the brown eyes of his "big brother," but he felt shy upon so solemn a subject.)

"Me! Lor', yes, some day I will marry." He smiled, did the always contemptuous Yann, rolling his passionate eyes. "But I'll have none of the lasses at home; no, I'll wed the sea, and I invite ye all in the barkey now, to the ball I'll give at my wedding."

They kept on hauling in, for their time could not be lost in chatting; they had an immense quantity of fish in a traveling shoal, which had not ceased passing for the last two days.

They had been up all night, and in thirty hours had caught more than a thousand prime cods; so that even their strong arms were tired and they were half asleep. But their bodies remained active and they continued their toil, though occasionally their minds floated off into regions of profound sleep. But the free air they breathed was as pure as that of the first young days of the world, and so bracing, that notwithstanding their weariness they felt their chests expand and their cheeks glow as at arising.

Morning, the true morning light, at length came; as in the days of Genesis, it had "divided from the darkness," which had settled upon the horizon and rested there in great heavy masses; and by the clearness of vision now, it was seen night had passed, and that that first vague strange glimmer was only a forerunner. In the thickly-veiled heavens, broke out rents here and there, like side skylights in a dome, through which pierced glorious rays of light, silver and rosy. The lower-lying clouds were grouped round in a belt of intense shadow, encircling the waters and screening the far-off distance in darkness. They hinted as of a space in a boundary; they were as curtains veiling the infinite, or as draperies drawn to hide the too majestic mysteries, which would have perturbed the imagination of mortals.

On this special morning, around the small plank platform occupied by Yann and Sylvestre, the shifting outer world had an appearance of deep meditation, as though this were an altar recently raised; and the sheaves of sun-rays, which darted like arrows under the sacred arch, spread in a long glimmering stream over the motionless waves, as over a marble floor. Then, slowly and more slowly yet loomed still another wonder; a high, majestic, pink profile—it was a promontory of gloomy Iceland.

Yann's wedding with the sea? Sylvestre was still thinking of it—after resuming his fishing without daring to say anything more. He had felt quite sad when his big brother had so turned the holy sacrament of marriage into ridicule; and it particularly had frightened him, as he was superstitious.

For so long, too, he had mused on Yann's marriage! He had thought that it might take place with Gaud Mevel, a blonde lass from Paimpol; and that he would have the happiness of being present at the marriage-feast before starting for the navy, that long five years' exile, with its dubious return, the thought of which already plucked at his heart-strings.

Four o'clock in the morning now. The watch below came up, all three, to relieve the others. Still rather sleepy, drinking in chestfuls of the fresh, chill air, they stepped up, drawing their long sea-boots higher, and having to shut their eyes, dazzled at first by a light so pale, yet in such abundance.

Yann and Sylvestre took their breakfast of biscuits, which they had to break with a mallet, and began to munch noisily, laughing at their being so very hard. They had become quite merry again at the idea of going down to sleep, snugly and warmly in their berths; and clasping each other round the waist they danced up to the hatchway to an old song-tune.

Before disappearing through the aperture they stopped to play with Turc, the ship's dog, a young Newfoundland with great clumsy paws. They sparred at him, and he pretended to bite them like a young wolf, until he bit too hard and hurt them, whereupon Yann, with a frown and anger in his quick-changing eyes, pushed him aside with an impatient blow that sent him flying and made him howl. Yann had a kind heart enough, but his nature remained rather untamed, and when his physical being was touched, a tender caress was often more like a manifestation of brutal violence.

CHAPTER II—ICELANDERS

Their smack was named *La Marie*, and her master was Captain Guermeur. Every year she set sail for the big dangerous fisheries, in the frigid regions where the summers have no night. She was a very old ship, as old as the statuette of her patron saint itself. Her heavy, oaken planks were rough and worn, impregnated with ooze and brine, but still strong and stout, and smelling strongly of tar. At anchor she looked an old unwieldy tub from her so massive build, but when blew the mighty western gales, her lightness returned, like a sea-gull awakened by the wind. Then she had her own style of tumbling over the rollers, and rebounding more lightly than many newer ones, launched with all your new fangles.

As for the crew of six men and the boy, they were "Icelanders," the valiant race of seafarers whose homes are at Paimpol and Treguier, and who from father to son are destined for the cod fisheries.

They hardly ever had seen a summer in France. At the end of each winter they, with other fishers, received the parting blessing in the harbour of Paimpol. And for that fete-day an altar, always the same, and imitating a rocky grotto, was erected on the quay; and over it, in the midst of anchors, oars and nets, was enthroned the Virgin Mary, calm, and beaming with affection, the patroness of sailors; she would be brought from her chapel for the occasion, and had looked upon generation after generation with her same lifeless eyes, blessing the happy for whom the season would be lucky, and the others who never more would return.

The Host, followed by a slow procession of wives, mothers, sweethearts, and sisters, was borne round the harbour, where the boats bound for Iceland, bedecked in all colours, saluted it on its way. The priest halted before each, giving them his holy blessing; and then the fleet started, leaving the country desolate of husbands, lovers, and sons; and as the shores faded from their view, the crews sang together in low, full voices, the hymns sacred to "the Star of the Ocean." And every year saw the same ceremonies, and heard the same good-byes.

Then began the life out upon the open sea, in the solitude of three or four rough companions, on the moving thin planks in the midst of the seething waters of the northern seas.

Until now *La Marie* followed the custom of many Icelanders, which is merely to touch at Paimpol, and then to sail down to the Gulf of Gascony, where fish fetches high prices, or farther on to the Sandy Isles, with their salty swamps, where they buy the salt for the next expedition. The crews of lusty fellows stay a few days in the southern, sun-kissed harbour-towns, intoxicated by the last rays of summer, by the sweetness of the balmy air, and by the downright jollity of youth.

With the mists of autumn they return home to Paimpol, or to the scattered huts of the land of Goelo, to remain some time in their families, in the midst of love, marriages, and births. Very often they find unseen babies upon their return, waiting for godfathers ere they can be baptized, for many children are needed to keep up this race of fishermen, which the Icelandic Moloch devours.

CHAPTER III—THE WOMEN AT HOME

At Paimpol, one fine evening of this same year, upon a Sunday in June, two women were deeply busy in writing a letter. This took place before a large open window, with a row of flowerpots on its heavy old granite sill.

As well as could be seen from their bending over the table, both were young. Once wore a very large old-fashioned cap; the other quite a small one, in the new style adopted by the women of Paimpol. They might have been taken for two loving lasses writing a tender missive to some handsome Icelander.

The one who dictated—the one with the large head-dress—drew up her head, wool-gathering. Oh, she was old, very old, notwithstanding her look from behind, in her small brown shawl—we mean downright old. A sweet old granny, seventy at least. Very pretty, though, and still fresh-coloured, with the rosy cheeks some old people have. Her *coiffe* was drawn low upon the forehead and upon the top of the head, was composed of two or three large rolls of muslin that seemed to telescope out of one another, and fell on to the nape. Her venerable face, framed in the pure white pleats, had almost a man's look, while her soft, tender eyes wore a kindly expression. She had not the vestige of a tooth left, and when she laughed she showed her round gums, which had still the freshness of youth.

Although her chin had become as pointed "as the toe of a *sabot*" (as she was in the habit of saying), her profile was not spoiled by time; and it was easily imagined that in her youth it had been regular and pure, like the saints' adorning a church.

She looked through the window, trying to think of news that might amuse her grandson at sea. There existed not in the whole country of Paimpol another dear old body like her, to invent such funny stories upon everybody, and even upon nothing. Already in this letter there were three or four merry tales, but without the slightest mischief, for she had nothing ill-natured about her.

The other woman, finding that the ideas were getting scarce, began to write the address carefully:

"TO MONSIEUR MOAN, SYLVESTRE, ABOARD THE *MARIE*, co CAPTAIN GUERMEUR, IN THE SEA OF ICELAND, NEAR RYKAWYK."

Here she lifted her head to ask: "Is that all, Granny Moan?"

The querist was young, adorably young, a girl of twenty in fact; very fair —a rare complexion in this corner of Brittany, where the race runs swarthy—very fair, we say, with great grey eyes between almost black lashes; her brows, as fair as the hair, seemed as if they had a darker streak in their midst, which gave a wonderful expression of strength and will to the beautiful face. The rather short profile was very dignified, the nose continuing the line of the brow with absolute rectitude, as in a Greek statue. A deep dimple under the lower lip foiled it up delightfully; and from time to time, when she was absorbed by a particular idea, she bit this lower lip with her white upper teeth, making the blood run in tiny red veins under the delicate skin. In her supple form there was no little pride, with gravity also, which she inherited from the bold Icelandic sailors, her ancestors. The expression of her eyes was both steady and gentle.

Her cap was in the shape of a cockle-shell, worn low on the brow, and drawn back on either side, showing thick tresses of hair about the ears, a head-dress that has remained from remote times and gives quite an olden look to the women of Paimpol.

One felt instinctively that she had been reared differently than the poor old woman to whom she gave the name of grandmother, but who is reality was but a distant great-aunt.

She was the daughter of M. Mevel, a former Icelander, a bit of a freebooter, who had made a fortune by bold undertakings out at sea.

The fine room where the letter had been just written was hers; a new bed, such as townspeople have, with muslin lace-edged curtains, and on the stone walls a light-coloured paper, toning down the irregularities of the granite; overhead a coating of whitewash covered the great beams that revealed the antiquity of the abode; it was the home of well-to-do folk, and the windows looked out upon the old gray market-place of Paimpol, where the *pardons* are held.

"Is it done, Granny Yvonne? Have you nothing else to tell him?"

"No, my lass, only I would like you to add a word of greeting to young Gaos."

"Young Gaos" was otherwise called Yann. The proud beautiful girl had blushed very red when she wrote those words. And as soon as they were added at the bottom of the page, in a running hand, she rose and turned her head aside as if to look at some very interesting object out on the market-place.

Standing, she was rather tall; her waist was modelled in a clinging bodice, as perfectly fitting as that of a fashionable dame. In spite of her cap, she looked like a real lady. Even her hands, without being conventionally small, were white and delicate, never having touched rough work.

True, she had been at first little *Gaud* (Daisy), paddling bare-footed in the water, motherless, almost wholly neglected during the season of the fisheries, which her father spent in Iceland; a pretty, untidy, obstinate girl, but growing vigorous and strong in the bracing sea-breeze. In those days she had been sheltered, during the fine summers, by poor Granny Moan, who used to give her Sylvestre to mind during her days of hard work in Paimpol. Gaud felt the adoration of a young mother for the child confided to her tender care. She was his elder by about eighteen months. He was as dark as she was fair, as obedient and caressing as she was hasty and capricious. She well remembered that part of her life; neither wealth nor town life had altered it; and like a far-off dream of wild freedom it came back to her, or as the remembrance of an undefined and mysterious previous existence, where the sandy shores seemed longer, and the cliffs higher and nobler.

Towards the age of five or six, which seemed long ago to her, wealth had befallen her father, who began to buy and sell the cargoes of ships. She had been taken to Saint-Brieuc, and later to Paris. And from *la petite Gaud* she had become Mademoiselle Marguerite, tall and serious, with earnest eyes. Always left to herself, in another kind of solitude than that of the Breton coast, she still retained the obstinate nature of her childhood.

Living in large towns, her dress had become more modified than herself. Although she still wore the *coiffe* that Breton women discard so seldom, she had learned to dress herself in another way.

Every year she had returned to Brittany with her father—in the summer only, like a fashionable, coming to bathe in the sea—and lived again in the midst of old memories, delighted to hear herself called Gaud, rather curious to see the Icelanders of whom so much was said, who were never at home, and of whom, each year, some were missing; on all sides she heard the name of Iceland, which appeared to her as a distant insatiable abyss. And there, now, was the man she loved!

One fine day she had returned to live in the midst of these fishers, through a whim of her father, who had wished to end his days there, and live like a landsman in the market-place of Paimpol.

The good old dame, poor but tidy, left Gaud with cordial thanks as soon as the letter had been read again and the envelope closed. She lived rather far away, at the other end of Ploubazlanec, in a hamlet on the coast, in the same cottage where she first had seen the light of day, and where her sons and grandsons had been born. In the town, as she passed along, she answered many friendly nods; she was one of the oldest inhabitants of the country, the last of a worthy and highly esteemed family.

With great care and good management she managed to appear pretty well dressed, although her gowns were much darned, and hardly held together. She always wore the tiny brown Paimpol shawl, which was for best, and upon which the long muslin rolls of her white caps had fallen for past sixty years; her own marriage shawl, formerly blue, had been dyed for the wedding of her son Pierre, and since then worn only on Sundays, looked quite nice.

She still carried herself very straight, not at all like an old woman; and, in spite of her pointed chin, her soft eyes and delicate profile made all think her still very charming. She was held in great respect—one could see that if only by the nods that people gave her.

On her way she passed before the house of her gallant, the sweetheart of former days, a carpenter by trade; now an octogenarian, who sat outside his door all the livelong day, while the young ones, his sons, worked in the shop. It was said that he never had consoled himself for her loss, for neither in first or second marriage would she have him; but with old age his feeling for her had become a sort of comical spite, half friendly and half mischievous, and he always called out to her:

"Aha, *la belle*, when must I call to take your measure?"

But she declined with thanks; she had not yet quite decided to have that dress made. The truth is, that the old man, with rather questionable taste, spoke of the suit in deal planks, which is the last of all our terrestrial garments.

"Well, whenever you like; but don't be shy in asking for it, you know, old lady."

He had made this joke several times; but, to-day, she could scarcely take it good-naturedly. She felt more tired than ever of her hard-working life, and her thoughts flew back to her dear grandson—the last of them all, who, upon his return from Iceland, was to enter the navy for five years! Perhaps he might have to go to China, to the war! Would she still be about, upon his return? The thought alone was agony to her. No, she was surely not so happy as she looked, poor old granny!

And was it really possible and true, that her last darling was to be torn from her? She, perhaps, might die alone, without seeing him again! Certainly, some gentlemen of the town, whom she knew, had done all they could to keep him from having to start, urging that he was the sole support of an old and almost destitute grandmother, who could no longer work. But they had not succeeded—because of Jean Moan, the deserter, an elder brother of Sylvestre's, whom no one in the family ever mentioned now, but who still lived somewhere over in America, thus depriving his younger brother of the military exemption. Moreover, it had been objected that she had her small pension, allowed to the widows of sailors, and the Admiralty could not deem her poor enough.

When she returned home, she said her prayers at length for all her dead ones, sons and grandsons; then she prayed again with renewed strength and confidence for her Sylvestre, and tried to sleep—thinking of the "suit of wood," her heart sadly aching at the thought of being so old, when this new parting was imminent.

Meanwhile, the other victim of separation, the girl, had remained seated at her window, gazing upon the golden rays of the setting sun, reflected on the granite walls, and the black swallows wheeling across the sky above. Paimpol was always quiet on these long May evenings, even on Sundays; the lasses, who had not a single lad to make love to them, sauntered along, in couples or three together, brooding of their lovers in Iceland.

"A word of greeting to young Gaos!" She had been greatly affected in writing that sentence, and that name, which now she could not forget. She often spent her evenings here at the window, like a grand lady. Her father did not approve of her walking with the other girls of her age, who had been her early playmates. And as he left the cafe, and walked up and down, smoking his pipe with old seamen like himself, he was happy to look up at his daughter among her flowers, in his grand house.

"Young Gaos!" Against her will she gazed seaward; it could not be seen, but she felt it was nigh, at the end of the tiny street crowded with fishermen. And her thoughts travelled through a fascinating and delightful infinite, far, far away to the northern seas, where "*La Marie,* Captain Guermeur," was sailing. A strange man was young Gaos! retiring and almost incomprehensible now, after having come forward so audaciously, yet so lovingly.

In her long reverie, she remembered her return to Brittany, which had taken place the year before. One December morning after a night of travelling, the train from Paris had deposited her father and herself at

Guingamp. It was a damp, foggy morning, cold and almost dark. She had been seized with a previously unknown feeling; she could scarcely recognise the quaint little town, which she had only seen during the summer—oh, that glad old time, the dear old times of the past! This silence, after Paris! This quiet life of people, who seemed of another world, going about their simple business in the misty morning. But the sombre granite houses, with their dark, damp walls, and the Breton charm upon all things, which fascinated her now that she loved Yann, had seemed particularly saddening upon that morning. Early housewives were already opening their doors, and as she passed she could glance into the old-fashioned houses, with their tall chimney-pieces, where sat the old grandmothers, in their white caps, quiet and dignified. As soon as daylight had begun to appear, she had entered the church to say her prayers, and the grand old aisle had appeared immense and shadowy to her—quite different from all the Parisian churches—with its rough pillars worn at the base by the chafing of centuries, and its damp, earthy smell of age and saltpetre.

In a damp recess, behind the columns, a taper was burning, before which knelt a woman, making a vow; the dim flame seemed lost in the vagueness of the arches. Gaud experienced there the feeling of a long-forgotten impression: that kind of sadness and fear that she had felt when quite young at being taken to mass at Paimpol Church on raw, wintry mornings.

But she hardly regretted Paris, although there were many splendid and amusing sights there. In the first place she felt almost cramped from having the blood of the vikings in her veins. And then, in Paris, she felt like a stranger and an intruder. The *Parisiennes* were tight-laced, artificial women, who had a peculiar way of walking; and Gaud was too intelligent even to have attempted to imitate them. In her head-dress, ordered every year from the maker in Paimpol, she felt out of her element in the capital; and did not understand that if the wayfarers turned round to look at her, it was only because she made a very charming picture.

Some of these Parisian ladies quite won her by their high-bred and distinguished manners, but she knew them to be inaccessible to her, while from others of a lower caste who would have been glad to make friends with her, she kept proudly aloof, judging them unworthy of her attention. Thus she had lived almost without friends, without other society than her father's, who was engaged in business and often away. So she did not regret that life of estrangement and solitude.

But, none the less, on that day of arrival she had been painfully surprised by the bitterness of this Brittany, seen in full winter. And her heart sickened at the thought of having to travel another five or six hours in a jolting car—to penetrate still farther into the blank, desolate country to reach Paimpol.

All through the afternoon of that same grisly day, her father and herself had journeyed in a little old ramshackle vehicle, open to all the winds; passing, with the falling night, through dull villages, under ghostly trees, black-pearled with mist in drops. And ere long lanterns had to be lit, and she could perceive nothing else but what seemed two trails of green Bengal lights, running on each side before the horses, and which were merely the beams that the two lanterns projected on the never-ending hedges of the roadway. But how was it that trees were so green in the month of December? Astonished at first, she bent to look out, and then she remembered how the gorse, the evergreen gorse of the paths and the cliffs, never fades in the country of Paimpol. At the same time a warmer breeze began to blow, which she knew again and which smelt of the sea.

Towards the end of the journey she had been quite awakened and amused by the new notion that struck her, namely: "As this is winter, I shall see the famous fishermen of Iceland."

For in December they were to return, the brothers, cousins, and lovers of whom all her friends, great and small, had spoken to her during the long summer evening walks in her holiday trips. And the thought had haunted her, though she felt chilled in the slow-going vehicle.

Now she had seen them, and her heart had been captured by one of them too.

CHAPTER IV—FIRST LOVE

The first day she had seen him, this Yann, was the day after his arrival, at the "*Pardon des Islandais,*" which is on the eighth of December, the fete-day of Our Lady of Bonne-Nouvelle, the patroness of fishers—a little before the procession, with the gray streets, still draped in white sheets, on which were strewn ivy and holly and wintry blossoms with their leaves.

At this *Pardon* the rejoicing was heavy and wild under the sad sky. Joy without merriment, composed chiefly of insouciance and contempt; of physical strength and alcohol; above which floated, less disguised than elsewhere, the universal warning of death.

A great clamour in Paimpol; sounds of bells mingled with the chants of the priests. Rough and monotonous songs in the taverns—old sailor lullabies—songs of woe, arisen from the sea, drawn from the deep night of bygone ages. Groups of sailors, arm-in-arm, zigzagging through the streets, from their habit of rolling, and because they were half-drunk. Groups of girls in their nun-like white caps. Old granite houses sheltering these seething crowds; antiquated roofs telling of their struggles, through many centuries, against the western winds, the mist, and the rain; and relating, too, many stories of love and adventure that had passed under their protection.

And floating over all was a deep religious sentiment, a feeling of bygone days, with respect for ancient veneration and the symbols that protect it, and for the white, immaculate Virgin. Side by side with the taverns rose the church, its deep sombre portals thrown open, and steps strewn with flowers, with its perfume of incense, its lighted tapers, and the votive offerings of sailors hung all over the sacred arch. And side by side also with the happy girls were the sweethearts of dead sailors, and the widows of the shipwrecked fishers, quitting the chapel of the dead in their long mourning shawls and their smooth tiny *coiffes*; with eyes downward bent, noiselessly they passed through the midst of this clamouring life, like a sombre warning. And close to all was the everlasting sea, the huge nurse and devourer of these vigorous generations, become fierce and agitated as if to take part in the fete.

Gaud had but a confused impression of all these things together. Excited and merry, yet with her heart aching, she felt a sort of anguish seize her at the idea that this country had now become her own again. On the market-place, where there were games and acrobats, she walked up and down with her friends, who named and pointed out to her from time to time the young men of Paimpol or Ploubazlanec. A group of these "Icelanders" were standing before the singers of "*complaintes*," (songs of woe) with their backs turned towards them. And directly Gaud was struck with one of them, tall as a giant, with huge shoulders almost too broad; but she had simply said, perhaps with a touch of mockery: "There is one who is tall, to say the least!" And the sentence implied beneath this was: "What an incumbrance he'll be to the woman he marries, a husband of that size!"

He had turned round as if he had heard her, and had given her a quick glance from top to toe, seeming to say: "Who is this girl who wears the *coiffe* of Paimpol, who is so elegant, and whom I never have seen before?"

And he quickly bent his eyes to the ground for politeness' sake, and had appeared to take a renewed interest in the singers, only showing the back of his head and his black hair that fell in rather long curls upon his neck. And although she had asked the names of several others, she had not dared ask his. The fine profile, the grand half-savage look, the brown, almost tawny pupils moving rapidly on the bluish opal of the eyes; all this had impressed her and made her timid.

And it just happened to be that "Fils Gaos," of whom she had heard the Moans speak as a great friend of Sylvestre's. On the evening of this same *Pardon*, Sylvestre and he, walking arm-in-arm, had crossed her father and herself, and had stopped to wish them good-day.

And young Sylvestre had become again to her as a sort of brother. As they were cousins they had continued to *tutoyer* (using thou for you, a sign of familiarity) each other; true, she had at first hesitated doing so to this great boy of seventeen, who already wore a black beard, but as his kind, soft, childish eyes had hardly changed at all, she recognized him soon enough to imagine that she had never lost sight of him.

When he used to come into Paimpol, she kept him to dinner of an evening; it was without consequence to her, and he always had a very good appetite, being on rather short rations at home.

To speak truly, Yann had not been very polite to her at this first meeting, which took place at the corner of a tiny gray street, strewn with green branches. He had raised his hat to her, with a noble though timid gesture; and after having given her an ever-rapid glance, turned his eyes away, as if he were vexed with this meeting and in a hurry to go. A strong western breeze that had arisen during the procession, had scattered branches of box everywhere and loaded the sky with dark gray draperies.

Gaud, in her dreamland of remembrances, saw all this clearly again; the sad gloaming falling upon the remains of the *Pardon*; the sheets strewn with white flowers floating in the wind along the walls; the noisy groups of Icelanders, other waifs of the gales and tempests flocking into the taverns, singing to cheer themselves under the gloom of the coming rain; and above all, Gaud remembered the giant standing in front of her, turning aside as if annoyed, and troubled at having met her.

What a wonderful change had come over her since then; and what a difference there was between that hubbub and the present tranquility! How quiet and empty Paimpol seemed to-night in the warm long twilight of May, which kept her still at her window alone, lulled in her love's young dream!

CHAPTER V—THE SECOND MEETING

Their second meeting was at a wedding-feast. Young Gaos had been chosen to offer her his arm. At first she had been rather vexed, not liking the idea of strolling through the streets with this tall fellow, whom everybody would stare at, on account of his excessive height, and who, most probably, would not know what to speak to her about. Besides, he really frightened her with his wild, lofty look.

At the appointed hour all were assembled for the wedding procession save Yann, who had not appeared. Time passed, yet he did not come, and they talked of giving up any further waiting for him. Then it was she discovered that it was for his pleasure, and his alone, that she had donned her best dress; with any other of the young men present at the ball, the evening's enjoyment would be spoiled.

At last he arrived, in his best clothes also, apologizing, without any embarrassment, to the bride's party. The excuse was, that some important shoals of fish, not at all expected, had been telegraphed from England, as bound to pass that night a little off Aurigny; and so all the boats of Ploubazlanec hastily had set sail. There was great excitement in the villages, women rushing about to find their husbands and urging them to put off quickly, and struggling hard themselves to hoist the sails and help in the launching; in fact, a regular "turnout" throughout the places, though in the midst of the company Yann related this very simply; he had been obliged to look out for a substitute and warrant him to the owner of the boat to which he belonged for the winter season. It was this that had caused him to be late, and in order not to miss the wedding, he had "turned up" (abandoned) his share in the profits of the catch. His plea was perfectly well understood by his hearers, no one thinking of blaming him; for well all know that, in this coast life, all are more or less dependent upon the unforeseen events at sea, and the mysterious migrations of the fishy regions. The other Icelandes present were disappointed at not having been warned in time, like the fishers of Ploubazlanec, of the fortune that was skirting their very shores.

But it was too late now, worse luck! So they gave their arms to the lasses, the violins began to play, and joyously they all tramped out.

At first Yann had only paid her a few innocent compliments, such as fall to a chance partner met at a wedding, and of whom one knows but little. Amidst all the couples in the procession, they formed the only one of strangers, the others were all relatives or sweethearts.

But during the evening while the dancing was going on, the talk between them had again turned to the subject of the fish, and looking her straight in the eyes, he roughly said to her:

"You are the only person about Paimpol, and even in the world, for whom I would have missed a windfall; truly, for nobody else would I have come back from my fishing, Mademoiselle Gaud."

At first she was rather astonished that this fisherman should dare so to address her who had come to this ball rather like a young queen, but then delighted, she had ended by answering:

"Thank you, Monsieur Yann; and I, too, would rather be with you than with anybody else."

That was all. But from that moment until the end of the dancing, they kept on chatting in a different tone than before, low and soft-voiced.

The dancing was to the sound of a hurdy-gurdy and violin, the same couples almost always together. When Yann returned to invite her again, after having danced with another girl for politeness' sake, they exchanged a smile, like friends meeting anew, and continued their interrupted conversation, which had become very close. Simply enough, Yann spoke of his fisher life, its hardships, its wage, and of his parents' difficulties in former years, when they had fourteen little Gaoses to bring up, he being the eldest. Now, the old folks were out of the reach of need, because of a wreck that their father had found in the Channel, the sale of which had brought in 10,000 francs, omitting the share claimed by the Treasury. With the money they built an upper story to their house, which was situated at the point of Ploubazlanec, at the very land's end, in the hamlet of Pors-Even, overlooking the sea, and having a grand outlook.

"It is mighty tough, though," said he, "this here life of an Icelander, having to start in February for such a country, where it is awful cold and bleak, with a raging, foaming sea."

Gaud remembered every phrase of their conversation at the ball, as if it had all happened yesterday, and details came regularly back to her mind, as she looked upon the night falling over Paimpol. If Yann had had no idea of marriage, why had he told her all the items of his existence, to which she had listened, as only an engaged sweetheart would have done; he did not seem a commonplace young man, prone to babbling his business to everybody who came along.

"The occupation is pretty good, nevertheless," he said, "and I shall never change my career. Some years we make eight hundred francs, and others twelve hundred, which I get upon my return, and hand over to the old lady."

"To your mother, Monsieur Yann, eh?"

"Yes, every penny of it, always. It's the custom with us Icelanders, Mademoiselle Gaud." He spoke of this as a quite ordinary and natural course.

"Perhaps you'll hardly believe it, but I scarcely ever have any pocket-money. Of a Sunday mother gives me a little when I come into Paimpol. And so it goes all the time. Why, look 'ee here, this year my father had these clothes made for me, without which treat I never could have come to the wedding; certain sure, for I never should have dared offer you my arm in my old duds of last year."

For one like her, accustomed to seeing Parisians, Yann's habiliments were, perhaps, not very stylish; a short jacket open over the old-fashioned waistcoat; but the build of their wearer was irreproachably handsome, so that he had a noble look withal.

Smiling, he looked at her straight in the depths of her eyes each time he spoke to her, so as to divine her opinion. And how good and honest was his look, as he told her all these short-comings, so that she might well understand that he was not rich!

And she smiled also, as she gazed at him full in the face; answering seldom, but listening with her whole soul, more and more astonished and more and more drawn towards him. What a mixture of untamed roughness and caressing childishness he was! His earnest voice, short and blunt towards others, became softer and more and more tender as he spoke to her; and for her alone he knew how to make it trill with extreme sweetness, like the music of a stringed instrument with the mute upon it.

What a singular and astonishing fact it was to see this man of brawn, with his free air and forbidding aspect, always treated by his family like a child, and deeming it quite natural; having travelled over all the earth, met with all sorts of adventures, incurred all dangers, and yet showing the same respectful and absolute obedience to his parents.

She compared him to others, two or three dandies in Paris, clerks, quill-drivers, or what not, who had pestered her with their attentions, for the sake of her money. He seemed to be the best, as well as the most handsome, man she had ever met.

To put herself more on an equality with him she related how, in her own home, she had not always been so well-off as at present; that her father had begun life as a fisherman off Iceland, and always held the Icelanders in great esteem; and that she herself could clearly remember as a little child, having run barefooted upon the beach, after her poor mother's death.

Oh! the exquisite night of that ball, unique in her life! It seemed far away now, for it dated back to December, and May had already returned. All the sturdy partners of that evening were out fishing yonder now, scattered over the far northern seas, in the clear pale sun, in intense loneliness, while the dust thickened silently on the land of Brittany.

Still Gaud remained at her window. The market-place of Paimpol, hedged in on all sides by the old-fashioned houses, became sadder and sadder with the darkling; everywhere reigned silence. Above the housetops the still brilliant space of the heavens seemed to grow more hollow, to raise itself up and finally separate itself from all terrestrial things: these, in the last hour of day, were entirely blended into the single dark outline of the gables of olden roofs.

From time to time a window or door would be suddenly closed; some old sailor, shaky upon his legs, would blunder out of the tavern and plunge into the small dark streets; or girls passed by, returning home late after their walk and carrying nosegays of May-flowers. One of them who knew Gaud, calling out good-evening to her, held up a branch of hawthorn high towards her as if to offer it her to smell; in the transparent darkness she could distinguish the airy tufts of its white blossoms. From the gardens and courts floated another soft perfume, that of the flowering honeysuckle along the granite walls, mingled with a vague smell of seaweed in the harbour.

Bats flew silently through the air above, like hideous creatures in a dream.

Many and many an evening had Gaud passed at her window, gazing upon the melancholy market-place, thinking of the Icelanders who were far away, and always of that same ball.

Yann was a capital waltzer, as straight as a young oak, moving with a graceful yet dignified bearing, his head thrown well back, his brown, curled locks falling upon his brow, and floating with the motion of the dance. Gaud, who was rather tall herself, felt their contact upon her cap, as he bent towards her to grasp her more tightly during the swift movements.

Now and then he pointed out to her his little sister Marie, dancing with Sylvestre, who was her *fiance*. He smiled with a very tender look at seeing them both so young and yet so reserved towards one another, bowing gravely, and putting on very timid airs as they communed lowly, on most amiable subjects, no doubt.

Of course, Yann would never have allowed it to be otherwise; yet it amused him, venturesome and bold as he was, to find them so coy; and he and Gaud exchanged one of their confidential smiles, seeming to say: "How pretty, but how funny *our* little brother is!"

Towards the close of the evening, all the girls received the breaking-up kiss; cousins, betrothed, and lovers, all, in a good frank, honest way, before everybody. But, of course, Yann had not kissed Gaud; none might take that liberty with the daughter of M. Mevel; but he seemed to strain her a little more tightly to him during the last waltzes, and she, trusting him, did not resist, but yielded closer still, giving up her whole soul, in the sudden, deep, and joyous attraction that bound her to him.

"Did you see the saucy minx, what eyes she made at him?" queried two or three girls, with their own eyes timidly bent under their golden or black brows, though they had among the dancers one or two lovers, to say the least. And truly Gaud did look at Yann very hard, only she had the excuse that he was the first and only young man whom she ever had noticed in her life.

At dawn, when the party broke up and left in confusion, they had taken leave of one another, like betrothed ones, who are sure to meet the following day. To return home, she had crossed this same market-place with her father, little fatigued, feeling light and gay, happy to breathe the frosty fog, and loving the sad dawn itself, so sweet and enjoyable seemed bare life.

The May night had long since fallen; nearly all the windows had closed with a grating of their iron fittings, but Gaud remained at her place, leaving hers open. The last passers-by, who could distinguish the white cap in the darkness, might say to themselves, "That's surely some girl, dreaming of her sweetheart." It was true, for she was dreaming of hers, with a wild desire to weep; her tiny teeth bit her lips and continually opened and pursed up the deep dimple that outlined the under lip of her fresh, pure mouth. Her eyes remained fixed on the darkness, seeing nothing of tangible things.

But, after the ball, why had he not returned? What change had come over him? Meeting him by chance, he seemed to avoid her, turning aside his look, which was always fleeting, by the way. She had often debated this with Sylvestre, who could not understand either.

"But still, he's the lad for you to marry, Gaud," said Sylvestre, "if your father allowed ye. In the whole country round you'd not find his like. First, let me tell 'ee, he's a rare good one, though he mayn't look it. He seldom gets tipsy. He sometimes is stubborn, but is very pliable for all that. No, I can't tell 'ee how good he is! And such an A.B. seaman! Every new fishing season the skippers regularly fight to have him."

She was quite sure of her father's permission, for she never had been thwarted in any of her whims. And it mattered little to her whether Yann were rich or not. To begin with, a sailor like him would need but a little money in advance to attend the classes of the coast navigation school, and might shortly become a captain whom all shipowners would gladly intrust with their vessels. It also mattered little to her that he was such a giant; great strength may become a defect in a woman, but in a man is not prejudicial to good looks.

Without seeming to care much, she had questioned the girls of the country round about, who knew all the love stories going; but he had no recognized engagement with any one, he paid no more attention to one than another, but roved from right to left, to Lezardrieux as well as to Paimpol, to all the beauties who cared to receive his address.

One Sunday evening, very late, she had seen him pass under her windows, in company with one Jeannie Caroff, whom he tucked under his wing very closely; she was pretty, certainly, but had a very bad reputation. This had pained Gaud very much indeed. She had been told that he was very quick-tempered: one night being rather tipsy in a tavern of Paimpol, where the Icelanders held their revels, he had thrown a great marble table through a door that they would not open to him. But she forgave him all that; we all know what sailors are sometimes when the fit takes them. But if his heart were good, why had he sought one out who never had thought of him, to leave her afterward; what reason had he had to look at her for a whole evening with his fair, open smile, and to use his softest, tenderest voice to speak to her of his affairs as to a betrothed? Now, it was impossible for her to become attached to another, or to change. In this same country, when quite a child, she was used to being scolded when naughty and called more stubborn than any other child in her ideas; and she had not altered. Fine lady as she was now, rather serious and proud in her ways, none had refashioned her, and she remained always the same.

After this ball, the past winter had been spent in waiting to see him again, but he had not even come to say good-bye before his departure for Iceland. Since he was no longer by, nothing else existed in her eyes; slowly time seemed to drag until the return in autumn, when she had made up her mind to put an end to her doubts.

The town-hall clock struck eleven, with that peculiar resonance that bells have during the quiet spring nights. At Paimpol eleven o'clock is very late; so Gaud closed her window and lit her lamp, to go to bed.

Perhaps it was only shyness in Yann, after all, or was it because, being proud also, he was afraid of a refusal, as she was so rich? She wanted to ask him this herself straightforwardly, but Sylvestre thought that it would not be the right thing, and it would not look well for her to appear so bold. In Paimpol already her manners and dress were sufficiently criticised.

She undressed slowly as if in a dream; first her muslin cap, then her town-cut dress, which she threw carelessly on a chair. The little lamp, alone to burn at this late hour, bathed her shoulders and bosom in its mysterious light, her perfect form, which no eye ever had contemplated, and never could contemplate if Yann did not marry her. She knew her face was beautiful, but she was unconscious of the beauty of her figure. In this remote land, among daughters of fishers, beauty of shape is almost part of the race; it is scarcely ever noticed, and even the least respectable women are ashamed to parade it.

Gaud began to unbraid her tresses, coiled in the shape of a snail-shell and rolled round her ears, and two plaits fell upon her shoulders like weighty serpents. She drew them up into a crown on the top of her head—this was comfortable for sleeping—so that, by reason of her straight profile, she looked like a Roman vestal.

She still held up her arms, and biting her lip, she slowly ran her fingers through the golden mass, like a child playing with a toy, while thinking of something else; and again letting it fall, she quickly unplaited it to spread it out; soon she was covered with her own locks, which fell to her knees, looking like some Druidess.

And sleep having come, notwithstanding love and an impulse to weep, she threw herself roughly in her bed, hiding her face in the silken masses floating round her outspread like a veil.

In her hut in Ploubazlanec, Granny Moan, who was on the other and darker side of her life, had also fallen to sleep—the frozen sleep of old age—dreaming of her grandson and of death.

And at this same hour, on board the *Marie*, on the Northern Sea, which was very heavy on this particular evening, Yann and Sylvestre—the two longed-for rovers—sang ditties to one another, and went on gaily with their fishing in the everlasting daylight.

CHAPTER VI—NEWS FROM HOME

About a month later, around Iceland, the weather was of that rare kind that the sailors call a dead calm; in other words, in the air nothing moved, as if all the breezes were exhausted and their task done.

The sky was covered with a white veil, which darkened towards its lower border near the horizon, and gradually passed into dull gray leaden tints; over this the still waters threw a pale light, which fatigued the eyes and chilled the gazer through and through. All at once, liquid designs played over the surface, such light evanescent rings as one forms by breathing on a mirror. The sheen of the waters seemed covered with a net of faint patterns, which intermingled and reformed, rapidly disappearing. Everlasting night or everlasting day, one could scarcely say what it was; the sun, which pointed to no special hour, remained fixed, as if presiding over the fading glory of dead things; it appeared but as a mere ring, being almost without substance, and magnified enormously by a shifting halo.

Yann and Sylvestre, leaning against one another, sang "Jean-Francois de Nantes," the song without an end; amused by its very monotony, looking at one another from the corner of their eyes as if laughing at the childish fun, with which they began the verses over and over again, trying to put fresh spirit into them each time. Their cheeks were rosy under the sharp freshness of the morning: the pure air they breathed was strengthening, and they inhaled it deep down in their chests, the very fountain of all vigorous existence. And yet, around them, was a semblance of non-existence, of a world either finished or not yet created; the light itself had no warmth; all things seemed without motion, and as if chilled for eternity under the great ghostly eye that represented the sun.

The *Marie* projected over the sea a shadow long and black as night, or rather appearing deep green in the midst of the polished surface, which reflected all the purity of the heavens; in this shadowed part, which had no glitter, could be plainly distinguished through the transparency, myriads upon myriads of fish, all alike, gliding slowly in the same direction, as if bent towards the goal of their perpetual travels. They were cod, performing their evolutions all as parts of a single body, stretched full length in the same direction, exactly parallel, offering the effect of gray streaks, unceasingly agitated by a quick motion that gave a look of fluidity to the mass of dumb lives. Sometimes, with a sudden quick movement of the tail, all turned round at the same time, showing the sheen of their silvered sides; and the same movement was repeated throughout the entire shoal by slow undulations, as if a thousand metal blades had each thrown a tiny flash of lightning from under the surface.

The sun, already very low, lowered further; so night had decidedly come. As the great ball of flame descended into the leaden-coloured zones that surrounded the sea, it grew yellow, and its outer rim became more clear and solid. Now it could be looked straight at, as if it were but the moon. Yet it still gave out light and looked quite near in the immensity; it seemed that by going in a ship, only so far as the edge of the horizon, one might collide with the great mournful globe, floating in the air just a few yards above the water.

Fishing was going on well; looking into the calm water, one could see exactly what took place; how the cod came to bite, with a greedy spring; then, feeling themselves hooked, wriggled about, as if to hook themselves still firmer. And every moment, with rapid action, the fishermen hauled in their lines, hand overhand, throwing the fish to the man who was to clean them and flatten them out.

The Paimpol fleet were scattered over the quiet mirror, animating the desert. Here and there appeared distant sails, unfurled for mere form's sake, considering there was no breeze. They were like clear white outlines upon the greys of the horizon. In this dead calm, fishing off Iceland seemed so easy and tranquil a trade that ladies' yachting was no name for it.

"Jean Francois de Nantes; Jean Francois, Jean Francois!"

So they sang, like a couple of children.

Yann little troubled whether or no he was handsome and good-looking. He was boyish only with Sylvestre, it is true, and sang and joked with no other; on the contrary, he was rather distant with the others and proud and disdainful—very willing though, when his help was required, and always kind and obliging when not irritated.

So the twain went on singing their song, with two others, a few steps off, singing another, a dirge—a clashing of sleepiness, health, and vague melancholy. But they did not feel dull, and the hours flew by.

Down in the cabin a fire still smouldered in the iron range, and the hatch was kept shut, so as to give the appearance of night there for those who needed sleep. They required but little air to sleep; indeed, less robust fellows, brought up in towns, would have wanted more. They used to go to bed after the watch at irregular times, just when they felt inclined, hours counting for little in this never-fading light. And they always slept soundly and peacefully without restlessness or bad dreams.

"Jean Francois de Nantes; Jean Francois, Jean Francois!"

They looked attentively at some almost imperceptible object, far off on the horizon, some faint smoke rising from the waters like a tiny jot of another gray tint slightly darker than the sky's. Their eyes were used to plumbing depths, and they had seen it.

"A sail, a sail, thereaway!"

"I have an idea," said the skipper, staring attentively, "that it's a government cruiser coming on her inspection-round."

This faint smoke brought news of home to the sailors, and among others, a letter we wrote of, from an old grandam, written by the hand of a beautiful girl. Slowly the steamer approached till they perceived her black hull. Yes, it was the cruiser, making the inspection in these western fjords.

At the same time, a slight breeze sprang up, fresher yet to inhale, and began to tarnish the surface of the still waters in patches; it traced designs in a bluish green tint over the shining mirror, and scattering in trails, these fanned out or branched off like a coral tree; all very rapidly with a low murmur; it was like a signal of awakening foretelling the end of this intense torpor. The sky, its veil being rent asunder, grew clear; the vapours fell down on the horizon, massing in heaps like slate-coloured wadding, as if to form a soft bank to the sea. The two ever-during mirrors between which the fishermen lived, the one on high and the one beneath, recovered their deep lucidity, as if the mists tarnishing them had been brushed away.

The weather was changing in a rapid way that foretold no good. Smacks began to arrive from all points of the immense plane; first, all the French smacks in the vicinity, from Brittany, Normandy, Boulogne, or Dunkirk. Like birds flocking to a call, they assembled round the cruiser; from the apparently empty corners of the horizon, others appeared on every side; their tiny gray wings were seen till they peopled the pallid waste.

No longer slowly drifting, for they had spread out their sails to the new and cool breeze, and cracked on all to approach.

Far-off Iceland also reappeared, as if she would fain come near them also; showing her great mountains of bare stones more distinctly than ever.

And there arose a new Iceland of similar colour, which little by little took a more definite form, and none the less was purely illusive, its gigantic mountains merely a condensation of mists. The sun, sinking low, seemed incapable of ever rising over all things, though glowing through this phantom island so tangible that it seemed placed in front of it. Incomprehensible sight! no longer was it surrounded by a halo, but its disc had become firmly spread, rather like some faded yellow planet slowly decaying and suddenly checked there in the heart of chaos.

The cruiser, which had stopped, was fully surrounded by the fleet of Icelanders. From all boats were lowered, like so many nut-shells, and conveyed their strong, long-bearded men, in barbaric-looking dresses, to the steamer.

Like children, all had something to beg for; remedies for petty ailments, materials for repairs, change of diet, and home letters. Others came, sent by their captains, to be clapped in irons, to expiate some fault; as they had all been in the navy, they took this as a matter of course. When the narrow deck of the cruiser was blocked-up by four or five of these hulking fellows, stretched out with the bilboes round their feet, the old sailor who had just chained them up called out to them, "Roll o' one side, my lads, to let us work, d'ye hear?" which they obediently did with a grin.

There were a great many letters this time for the Iceland fleet. Among the rest, two for "*La Marie*, Captain Guermeur"; one addressed to "Monsieur Gaos, Yann," the other to "Monsieur Moan, Sylvestre." The latter had come by way of Rykavyk, where the cruiser had taken it on.

The purser, diving into his post-bags of sailcloth, distributed them all round, often finding it hard to read the addresses, which were not always written very skilfully, while the captain kept on saying: "Look alive there, look alive! the barometer is falling."

He was rather anxious to see all the tiny yawls afloat, and so many vessels assembled in that dangerous region.

Yann and Sylvestre used to read their letters together. This time they read them by the light of the midnight sun, shining above the horizon, still like a dead luminary. Sitting together, a little to one side, in a retired nook of the deck, their arms about each other's shoulders, they very slowly read, as if to enjoy more thoroughly the news sent them from home.

In Yann's letter Sylvestre got news of Marie Gaos, his little sweetheart; in Sylvestre's, Yann read all Granny Moan's funny stories, for she had not her like for amusing the absent ones you will remember; and the last paragraph concerning him came up: the "word of greeting to young Gaos."

When the letters were got through, Sylvestre timidly showed his to his big friend, to try and make him admire the writing of it.

"Look, is it not pretty writing, Yann?"

But Yann, who knew very well whose hand had traced it, turned aside, shrugging his shoulders, as much as to say that he was worried too often about this Gaud girl.

So Sylvestre carefully folded up the poor, rejected paper, put it into its envelope and all in his jersey, next his breast, saying to himself sadly: "For sure, they'll never marry. But what on earth can he have to say against her?"

Midnight was struck on the cruiser's bell. And yet our couple remained sitting there, thinking of home, the absent ones, a thousand things in reverie. At this same moment the everlasting sun, which had dipped its lower edge into the waters, began slowly to reascend, and lo! this was morning.

PART II — IN THE BRETON LAND

CHAPTER I—THE PLAYTHING OF THE STORM

The Northern sun had taken another aspect and changed its colour, opening the new day by a sinister morn. Completely free from its veil, it gave forth its grand rays, crossing the sky in fitful flashes, foretelling nasty weather. During the past few days it had been too fine to last. The winds blew upon that swarm of boats, as if to clear the sea of them; and they began to disperse and flee, like an army put to rout, before the warning written in the air, beyond possibility to misread. Harder and harder it blew, making men and ships quake alike.

And the still tiny waves began to run one after another and to melt together; at first they were frosted over with white foam spread out in patches; and then, with a whizzing sound, arose smoke as though they burned and scorched, and the whistling grew louder every moment. Fish-catching was no longer thought of; it was their work on deck. The fishing lines had been drawn in, and all hurried to make sail and some to seek for shelter in the fjords, while yet others preferred to round the southern point of Iceland, finding it safer to stand for the open sea, with the free space about them, and run before the stern wind. They could still see each other a while: here and there, above the trough of the sea, sails wagged as poor wearied birds fleeing; the masts tipped, but ever and anon righted, like the weighted pith figures that similarly resume an erect attitude when released after being blown down.

The illimitable cloudy roof, erstwhile compacted towards the western horizon, in an island form, began to break up on high and send its fragments over the surface. It seemed indestructible, for vainly did the winds stretch it, pull and toss it asunder, continually tearing away dark strips, which they waved over the pale yellow sky, gradually becoming intensely and icily livid. Ever more strongly grew the wind that threw all things in turmoil.

The cruiser had departed for shelter at Iceland; some fishers alone remained upon the seething sea, which now took an ill-boding look and a dreadful colour. All hastily made preparations for bad weather. Between one and another the distance grew greater, till some were lost sight of.

The waves, curling up in scrolls, continued to run after each other, to reassemble and climb on one another, and between them the hollows deepened.

In a few hours, everything was belaboured and overthrown in these regions that had been so calm the day before, and instead of the past silence, the uproar was deafening. The present agitation was a dissolving view, unconscientious and useless, and quickly accomplished. What was the object of it all? What a mystery of blind destruction it was!

The clouds continued to stream out on high, out of the west continually, racing and darkening all. A few yellow clefts remained, through which the sun shot its rays in volleys. And the now greenish water was striped more thickly with snowy froth.

By midday the *Marie* was made completely snug for dirty weather: her hatches battened down, and her sails storm-reefed; she bounded lightly and elastic; for all the horrid confusion, she seemed to be playing like the porpoises, also amused in storms. With her foresail taken in, she simply scudded before the wind.

It had become quite dark overhead, where stretched the heavily crushing vault. Studded with shapeless gloomy spots, it appeared a set dome, unless a steadier gaze ascertained that everything was in the full rush of motion; endless gray veils were drawn along, unceasingly followed by others, from the profundities of the sky-line—draperies of darkness, pulled from a never-ending roll.

The *Marie* fled faster and faster before the wind; and time fled also—before some invisible and mysterious power. The gale, the sea, the *Marie*, and the clouds were all lashed into one great madness of hasty flight towards the same point. The fastest of all was the wind; then the huge seething billows, heavier and slower, toiling after; and, lastly, the smack, dragged into the general whirl. The waves tracked her down with their white crests, tumbling onward in continual motion, and she—though always being caught up to and outrun—still managed to elude them by means of the eddying waters she spurned in her wake, upon which they vented their fury. In this similitude of flight the sensation particularly experienced was of buoyancy, the delight of being carried along without effort or trouble, in a springy sort of way. The *Marie* mounted over the waves without any shaking, as if the wind had lifted her clean up; and her subsequent descent was a slide. She almost slid backward, though, at times, the mountains lowering before her as if continuing to run, and then she suddenly found herself dropped into one of the measureless hollows that evaded her also; without injury she sounded its horrible depths, amid a loud splashing of water, which did not even sprinkle her decks, but was blown on and on like everything else, evaporating in finer and finer spray until it was thinned away to nothing. In the trough it was darker, and when each wave had passed the men looked behind them to see if the next to appear were higher; it came upon them with furious contortions, and curling crests, over its transparent emerald body, seeming to shriek: "Only let me catch you, and I'll swallow you whole!"

But this never came to pass, for, as a feather, the billows softly bore them up and then down so gently; they felt it pass under them, with all its boiling surf and thunderous roar. And so on continually, but the sea getting heavier and heavier. One after another rushed the waves, more and more gigantic, like a long chain of mountains, with yawning valleys. And the madness of all this movement, under the ever-darkening sky, accelerated the height of the intolerable clamour.

Yann and Sylvestre stood at the helm, still singing, "Jean Francois de Nantes"; intoxicated with the quiver of speed, they sang out loudly, laughing at their inability to hear themselves in this prodigious wrath of the wind.

"I say, lads, does it smell musty up here too?" called out Guermeur to them, passing his bearded face up through the half-open hatchway, like Jack-in-the-box.

Oh, no! it certainly did not smell musty on deck. They were not at all frightened, being quite conscious of what men can cope with, having faith in the strength of their barkey and their arms. And they furthermore relied upon the protection of that china Virgin, which had voyaged forty years to Iceland, and so often had danced the dance of this day, smiling perpetually between her branches of artificial flowers.

Generally speaking, they could not see far around them; a few hundred yards off, all seemed entombed in the fearfully big billows, with their frothing crests shutting out the view. They felt as if in an enclosure, continually altering shape; and, besides, all things seemed drowned in the aqueous smoke, which fled before them like a cloud with the greatest rapidity over the heaving surface. But from time to time a gleam of sunlight pierced through the north-west sky, through which a squall threatened; a shuddering light would appear from above, a rather spun-out dimness, making the dome of the heavens denser than before, and feebly lighting up the surge. This new light was sad to behold; far-off glimpses as they were, that gave too strong an understanding that the same chaos and the same fury lay on all sides, even far, far behind the seemingly void horizon; there was no limit to its expanse of storm, and they stood alone in its midst!

A tremendous tumult arose all about, like the prelude of an apocalypse, spreading the terror of the ultimate end of the earth. And amidst it thousands of voices could be heard above, shrieking, bellowing, calling, as from a great distance. It was only the wind, the great motive breath of all this disorder, the voice of the invisible power ruling all. Then came other voices, nearer and less indefinite, threatening destruction, and making the water shudder and hiss as if on burning coals; the disturbance increased in terror.

Notwithstanding their flight, the sea began to gain on them, to "bury them up," as they phrased it: first the spray fell down on them from behind, and masses of water thrown with such violence as to break everything in their course. The waves were ever increasing, and the tempest tore off their ridges and hurled them, too, upon the poop, like a demon's game of snowballing, till dashed to atoms on the bulwarks. Heavier masses fell on the planks with a hammering sound, till the *Marie* shivered throughout, as if in pain. Nothing could be distinguished over the side, because of the screen of creamy foam; and when the winds soughed more loudly, this foam formed into whirling spouts, like the dust of the way in summer time. At length a heavy rain fell crossways, and soon straight up and down, and how all these elements of destruction yelled together, clashed and interlocked, no tongue can tell.

Yann and Sylvestre stuck staunchly to the helm, covered with their waterproofs, hard and shiny as sharkskin; they had firmly secured them at the throat by tarred strings, and likewise at wrists and ankles to prevent the water from running in, and the rain only poured off them; when it fell too heavily, they arched their backs, and held all the more stoutly, not to be thrown over the board. Their cheeks burned, and every minute their breath was beaten out or stopped.

After each sea was shipped and rushed over, they exchanged glances, grinning at the crust of salt settled in their beards.

In the long run though, this became tiresome, an unceasing fury, which always promised a worse visitation. The fury of men and beasts soon falls and dies away; but the fury of lifeless things, without cause or object, is as mysterious as life and death, and has to be borne for very long.

"Jean Francois de Nantes;

Jean Francois,

Jean Francois!"

Through their pale lips still came the refrain of the old song, but as from a speaking automaton, unconsciously taken up from time to time. The excess of motion and uproar had made them dumb, and despite their youth their smiles were insincere, and their teeth chattered with cold; their eyes, half-closed under their raw, throbbing eyelids, remained glazed in terror. Lashed to the helm, like marble caryatides, they only moved their numbed blue hands, almost without thinking, by sheer muscular habit. With their hair streaming and mouths contracted, they had become changed, all the primitive wildness in man appearing again. They could not see one another truly, but still were aware of being companioned. In the instants of greatest danger, each time that a fresh mountain of water rose behind them, came to overtower them, and crash horribly against their boat, one of their hands would move as if involuntarily, to form the sign of the cross. They no more thought of Gaud than of any other woman, or any marrying. The travail was lasting too long, and they had no thoughts left. The intoxication of noise, cold, and fatigue drowned all in their brain. They were merely two pillars of stiffened human flesh, held up by the helm; two strong beasts, cowering, but determined they would not be overwhelmed.

CHAPTER II—A PARDONABLE RUSE

In Brittany, towards the end of September, on an already chilly day, Gaud was walking alone across the common of Ploubazlanec, in the direction of Pors-Even.

The Icelanders had returned a month back, except two, which had perished in that June gale. But the *Marie* had held her own, and Yann and all her crew were peacefully at home.

Gaud felt very troubled at the idea of going to Yann's house. She had seen him once since the return from Iceland, when they had all gone together to see poor little Sylvestre off to the navy. They accompanied him to the coaching-house, he blubbering a little and his grandmother weeping, and he had started to join the fleet at Brest.

Yann, who had come also to bid good-bye to his little friend, had feigned to look aside when Gaud looked at him, and as there were many people round the coach to see the other sailors off, and parents assembled to say good-bye, the pair had not a chance to speak. So, at last, she had formed a strong resolution, and rather timidly wended her way towards the Gaos's home.

Her father had formerly had mutual interests with Yann's father (complicated business, which, with peasants and fishers alike, seems to be endless), and owed him a hundred francs for the sale of a boat, which had just taken place in a raffle.

"You ought to let me carry the money to him, father," she had said. "I shall be pleased to see Marie Gaos. I never have been so far in Ploubazlanec, either, and I shall enjoy the long walk."

To speak the truth, she was curiously anxious to know Yann's family, which she might some day enter; and she also wanted to see the house and village.

In one of their last chats, before his departure, Sylvestre had explained to her, in his own way, his friend's shyness.

"D'ye see, Gaud, he's like this, he won't marry anybody, that's his idea; he only loves the sea, and one day even, in fun, he said he had promised to be wedded to it."

Whereupon, she forgave him all his peculiar ways, and remembered only his beautiful open smile on the night of the ball, and she hoped on and on.

If she were to meet him in his home, of course she would say nothing; she had no intention of being so bold. But if he saw her closely again, perhaps he might speak.

CHAPTER III—OF SINISTER PORTENT

She had been walking for the last hour, lightly yet oppressed, inhaling the healthy open breeze whistling up the roads to where they crossed and *Calvaires* were erected, ghastly highway ornaments of our Saviour on His cross, to which Bretons are given.

From time to time she passed through small fishing villages, which are beaten about by the winds the whole year through till of the colour of the rocks. In one of these hamlets, where the path narrows suddenly between dark walls, and between the whitewashed roofs, high and pointed like Celtic huts, a tavern sign-board made her smile. It was "The Chinese Cider Cellars." On it were painted two grotesque figures, dressed in green and pink robes, with pigtails, drinking cider. No doubt the whim of some old sailor who had been in China. She saw all on her way; people who are greatly engrossed in the object of a journey always find more amusement than others in its thousand details.

The tiny village was far behind her now, and as she advanced in this last promontory of the Breton land, the trees around her became more scarce, and the country more mournful.

The ground was undulating and rocky, and from all the heights the open sea could be seen. No more trees now; nothing but the shorn heaths with their green reeds, and here and there the consecrated crosses rose, their outstretched arms outlined against the sky, giving the whole country the aspect of a cemetery.

At one of the cross-ways, guarded by a colossal image of Christ, she hesitated between two roads running among thorny slopes.

A child happening to pass, came to her rescue: "Good-day, Mademoiselle Gaud!"

It was one of the little Gaoses, one of Yann's wee sisters. Gaud kissed her and asked her if her parents were at home.

"Father and mother are, yes. But brother Yann," said the little one, without intent, of course, "has gone to Loguivy; but I don't think he'll be very late home again."

So he was not there? Again destiny was between them, everywhere and always. She thought at first of putting off her visit to another day. But the little lass who had met her might mention the fact. What would they think at Pors-Even? So she decided to go on, but loitering so as to give Yann time to return.

As she neared his village, in this lost country, all things seemed rougher and more desolate. Sea breezes that made men stronger, made shorter and more stubbly plants. Seaweeds of all kinds were scattered over the paths, leaves from growths in another element, proving the existence of a neighbouring world; their briny odour mingled with the perfume of the heather.

Now and again Gaud met passers-by, sea-folk, who could be seen a long way off, over the bare country, outlined and magnified against the high sea-line. Pilots or fishers, seeming to watch the great sea, in passing her wished her good-day. Broad sun-burnt faces were theirs, manly and determined under their easy caps.

Time did not go quickly enough, and she really did not know what to do to lengthen the way; these people seemed surprised at seeing her walk so slowly.

What could Yann be doing at Loguivy? Courting the girls, perhaps.

Ah! if she only had known how little he troubled his head about them! He had simply gone to Loguivy to give an order to a basket-maker, who was the only one in the country knowing how to weave lobster pots. His mind was very free from love just now.

She passed a chapel, at such a height it could be seen remotely. It was a little gray old chapel in the midst of the barren. A clump of trees, gray too, and almost leafless, seemed like hair to it, pushed by some invisible hand all on one side.

It was that same hand that had wrecked the fishers' boats, the eternal hand of the western winds, and had twisted all the branches of the coast trees in the direction of the waves and of the off-sea breezes. The old trees had grown awry and dishevelled, bending their backs under the time-honoured strength of that hand.

Gaud was almost at the end of her walk, as the chapel in sight was that of Pors-Even; so she stopped there to win a little more time.

A petty mouldering wall ran round an enclosure containing tombstones. Everything was of the same colour, chapel, trees, and graves; the whole spot seemed faded and eaten into by the sea-wind; the stones, the knotty branches, and the granite saints, placed in the wall niches, were covered by the same grayish lichen, splashed pale yellow.

On one of the wooden crosses this name was written in large letters:

"GAOS.—GAOS, JOEL, 80 years."

Yes, this was the old grandfather—she knew that—for the sea had not wanted this old sailor. And many of Yann's relatives, besides, slept here; it was only natural, and she might have expected it; nevertheless, the name upon the tomb had made a sad impression.

To waste a little more time, she entered to say a prayer under the old cramped porch, worn away and daubed over with whitewash. But she stopped again with a sharp pain at her heart. "Gaos"—again that name, engraved upon one of the slabs erected in memory of those who die at sea.

She read this inscription:

"To the Memory of GAOS, JEAN-LOUIS, Aged 24 years; seaman on board the *Marguerite*. Disappeared off Iceland, August 3d, 1877. May he rest in peace!"

Iceland—always Iceland! All over the porch were wooden slabs bearing the names of dead sailors. It was the place reserved for the shipwrecked of Pors-Even. Filled with a dark foreboding she was sorry to have gone there.

In Paimpol church she had seen many such inscriptions; but in this village the empty tomb of the Iceland fishers seemed more sad because so lone and humble. On each side of the doorway was a granite seat for the widows and mothers; and this shady spot, irregularly shaped like a grotto, was guarded by an old image of the Virgin, coloured red, with large staring eyes, looking most like Cybele—the first goddess of the earth.

"Gaos!" Again!

"To the Memory of GAOS, FRANCOIS, Husband of Anne-Marie le Goaster, Captain on board the *Paimpolais*, Lost off Iceland, between the 1st and 3d of May, 1877, With the twenty-three men of his crew. May they rest in peace!"

And, lower down, were two cross-bones under a black skull with green eyes, a simple but ghastly emblem, reminding one of all the barbarism of a bygone age.

"Gaos, Gaos!" The name was everywhere. As she read, thrills of sweet tenderness came over her for this Yann of her choice, damped by a feeling of hopelessness. Nay, he would never be hers! How could she tear him from the sea where so many other Gaoses had gone down, ancestors and brothers, who must have loved the sea like he! She entered the chapel. It was almost dark, badly lit by low windows with heavy frames. And there, her heart full of tears that would better have fallen, she knelt to pray before the colossal saints, surrounded by common flowers, touching the vaulted roof with their massive heads. Outside, the rising wind began to sob as if it brought the death-gasps of the drowned men back to their Fatherland.

Night drew near; she rose and went on her way. After having asked in the village, she found the home of the Gaos family, which was built up against a high cliff. A dozen granite steps led up to it. Trembling a little at the thought that Yann might have returned, she crossed the small garden where chrysanthemums and veronicas grew.

When she was indoors, she explained she had come to bring the money for the boat, and they very politely asked her to sit down, to await the father's return, as he was the one to sign the receipt for her. Amidst all, her eyes searched for Yann—but did not see him.

They were very busy in the home. Already they were cutting out the new waterproof cloth on the clean white table, and getting it ready for the approaching Iceland season.

"You see, Mademoiselle Gaud, it's like this: every man wants two new suits."

They explained to her how they set to work to make them, and to render their seams waterproof with tar, for they were for wet weather wear. And while they worked, Gaud looked attentively around the home of these Gaoses.

It was furnished after the traditional manner of all Breton cottages; an immense chimney-place took up one whole end, and on the sides of the walls the Breton beds, bunks, as on shipboard, were placed one above another. But it was not so sombre and sad as the cabins of other peasants, which are generally half-hidden by the wayside; it was all fresh and clean, as the homes of seamen usually are. Several little Gaoses were there, girls and boys, all sisters and brothers of Yann; without counting two big ones, who were already out at sea. And, besides, there was a little fair girl, neat, but sad, unlike the others.

"We adopted her last year," explained the mother; "we had enough children as it was, of course, but what else could we do, Mademoiselle Gaud, for her daddy belonged to the *Maria-Dieu-t'aime*, lost last season off Iceland, as you know; so the neighbours divided the little ones between them, and this one fell to our lot."

Hearing herself spoken of, the adopted child hung her pretty head and smiled, hiding herself behind little Laumec Gaos, her favourite.

There was a look of comfort all over the place, and radiant health bloomed on all the children's rosy cheeks.

They received Gaud very profusely, like a great lady whose visit was an honour to the family. She was taken upstairs, up a newly-built wooden staircase, to see the room above, which was the glory of the home. She remembered the history of its construction; it was after the finding of a derelict vessel in the channel, which luck had befallen Yann's father and his cousin the pilot.

The room was very gay and pretty in its whiteness; there were two town beds in it, with pink chintz curtains, and a large table in the middle. Through the window the whole of Paimpol could be seen, with the Icelanders at anchor off shore, and the channel through which they passed.

She did not dare question, but she would have liked to have known where Yann slept; probably as a child he had slept downstairs in one of the antique cupboard-beds. But perhaps now he slept under those pink draperies. She would have loved to have known all the details of his life, especially what he did in the long winter evenings.

A heavy footstep on the stairs made her tremble. But it was not Yann, though a man much like him; notwithstanding his white hair, as tall and as straight. It was old father Gaos returning from fishing.

After he had saluted her and asked her the object of her visit, he signed her receipt for her which was rather a long operation, as his hand was not very steady, he explained.

But he would not accept the hundred francs as a final payment, but only as an instalment; he would speak to M. Mevel again about it. Whereupon Gaud, to whom money was nothing, smiled imperceptibly; she had fancied the business was not quite terminated, and this just suited her.

They made something like excuses for Yann's absence; as if they found it more orthodox for the whole family to assemble to receive her. Perhaps the father had guessed, with the shrewdness of an old salt, that his son was not indifferent to this beautiful heiress; for he rather insisted upon talking about him.

"It's very queer," said he, "the boy's never so late out. He went over to Loguivy, Mademoiselle Gaud, to buy some lobster baskets; as you know, lobster-catching is our main winter fishery."

She dreamily lengthened out her call, although conscious that it was too long already, and feeling a tug at her heart at the idea that she would not see him after all.

"A well-conducted young man like Yann—what can he be doing? Surely he's not at the inn. We don't fear that for our lad. I don't say that now and then, of a Sunday, with his mates——You know, Mademoiselle Gaud, what them sailors are. Eh! ye know, he's but a young chap, and must have some liberty now and again. But it's very rare with him to break out, for he's a straight-goer; we can say that."

But night was falling, and the work had been folded up. The little ones on the benches around drew closer to one another, saddened by the grey dismal gloaming, and eyed Gaud hard, seeming to say—

"Why doesn't she go now?"

On the hearth, the flames burned redder in the midst of the falling shadows.

"You ought to stay and have a bit o' supper with us, Mademoiselle Gaud."

"Oh, no! I couldn't think of it!" The blood rushed to her face at the idea of having remained so late. She got up and took her leave.

Yann's father also rose to accompany her part of the way, anyhow as far as a lonely nook where the old trees make a dark lane.

As they walked along together, she felt a sudden sympathy of respect and tenderness towards him; she would have liked to have spoken as to a father in the sudden gushes of feeling that came over her; but the words were stifled in her throat, and she said not a word.

And so they went their way, in the cold evening wind, full of the odour of the sea, passing here and there, on the barren heath, some poor hovels, where beach-combers dwelt and had already sealed themselves up for the night; dark and neglected they looked under the weather-beaten roofs; these crosses, clumps of reeds, and boulders they left behind.

What a great way off Pors-Even was, and what a time she had remained!

Now and then they met folks returning from Paimpol or Loguivy; and as she watched the shadows approach, each time she thought it was Yann; but it was easy to recognise him at a good distance off, and so she was quickly undeceived. Every moment her feet caught in the brown trailing plants, tangled like hair, which were sea-weeds littering the pathway.

At the Cross of Plouezoc'h she bade good-bye to the old man, and begged him to return. The lights of Paimpol were already in view, and there was no more occasion to be afraid.

So hope was over for this time. Who could tell her when she might see Yann again?

An excuse to return to Pors-Even would have been easy; but it would really look too bad to begin her quest all over again. She would have to be braver and prouder than that. If only her little confidant Sylvestre had been there, she might have asked him to go and fetch Yann, so that there could be some explanation. But he was gone now, and for how many years?

CHAPTER IV—HIS RELUCTANCE

"Me get married?" said Yann to his parents that same evening. "Me get married? Good heavens, why should I? Shall I ever be as happy as here with ye? no troubles, no tiffs with any one, and warm soup ready for me every night when I come home from sea. Oh! I quite understand that you mean the girl that came here to-day, but what's such a rich girl to do with us? 'Tisn't clear to my thinking. And it'll be neither her, nor any other. It's all settled, I won't marry—it ain't to my liking."

The two old Gaoses looked at one another in silence, deeply disappointed, for, after having talked it over together, they were pretty well sure that this young lady would not refuse their handsome Yann. But they did not try to argue, knowing how useless that would be. The mother lowered her head, and said no more; she respected the will of her son, her eldest born, who was all but the head of the family; although he was always tender and gentle with her, more obedient than a child in the petty things of life, he long ago had been her absolute master for the great ones, eluding all restraint with a quiet though savage independence. He never sat up late, being in the habit, like other fishermen, of rising before break of day. And after supper at eight o'clock, he had given another satisfactory look to his baskets and new nets from Loguivy, and began to undress—calm to all appearances, and went up to sleep in the pink-curtained bed, which he shared with his little brother Laumec.

CHAPTER V—SAILORS AT THE PLAY

For the last fortnight Gaud's little confidant, Sylvestre, had been quartered in Brest; very much out of his element, but very quiet and obedient to discipline. He wore his open blue sailor-collar and red-balled, flat, woollen cap, with a frank, fearless look, and was noble and dignified in his sailor garb, with his free step and tall figure, but at the bottom of his heart he was still the same innocent boy as ever, and thinking of his dear old grandam.

One evening he had got tipsy together with some lads from his parts, simply because it is the custom; and they had all returned to the barracks together arm-in-arm, singing out as lustily as they could.

And one Sunday, too, they had all gone to the theatre, in the upper galleries. A melodrama was being played, and the sailors, exasperated against the villain, greeted him with a howl, which they all roared together, like a blast of the Atlantic cyclones.

CHAPTER VI—ORDERED ON FOREIGN SERVICE

One day Sylvestre was summoned before the officer of his company; and they told him he was among those ordered out to China—in the squadron for Formosa. He had been pretty well expecting it for some time, as he had heard those who read the papers say that out there the war seemed never-ending.

And because of the urgency of the departure, he was informed at the same time that he would not be able to have the customary leave for his home farewells; in five days' time he would have to pack up and be off.

Then a bitter pain came over him; though charmed at the idea of far-off travels amid the unknown and of the war. There also was agony at the thought of leaving all he knew and loved, with the vague apprehension that he might never more return.

A thousand noises rang in his head. Around was the bustle of the barrack-rooms, where hundreds of others were called up, like himself, chosen for the Chinese squadron. And rapidly he wrote to his old grandmother, with a stump of pencil, crouching on the floor, alone in his own feverish dream, though in the thick of the continual hurry and hubbub amidst all the young sailors hurried away like himself.

CHAPTER VII—MOAN'S SWEETHEART

"His sweetheart's a trifle old!" said the others, a couple of days later, as they laughed after Sylvestre and his grandmother, "but they seem to get on fine together all the same."

It amused them to see the boy, for the first time, walk through the streets of Recouvrance, with a woman at his side, like the rest of them; and, bending towards her with a tender look, whisper what seemed to be very soft nothings.

She was a very quick, diminutive person seen from behind, with rather short skirts for the fashion of the day; and a scanty brown shawl, and a high Paimpol *coiffe*. She, too, hanging on his arm, turned towards him with an affectionate glance.

"A trifle old was his sweetheart!"

That's what the others called after him, we say, but without spite, for any one could see that she was his old granny, come up from the country. She had come, too, in a hurry, suddenly terrified at the news of his sudden departure; for this Chinese war had already cost Paimpol many sailors. So she had scraped together all her poor little savings, put her best Sunday dress and a fresh clean *coiffe* in a box, and had set out to kiss him once again.

She had gone straight to the barracks to ask for him; at first his adjutant had refused to let him go out.

"If you've anything to say, my good woman, go and speak to the captain yourself. There he is, passing."

So she calmly walked up to him, and he allowed himself to be won over.

"Send Moan to change his clothes, to go out," said he.

All in hot haste Moan had gone to rig up in his best attire, while the good old lady, to make him laugh, of course, made a most inimitably droll face and a mock curtsey at the adjutant behind his back.

But when the grandson appeared in his full uniform, with the inevitable turned-down collar, leaving his throat bare, she was quite struck with his beauty; his black beard was cut into a seamanly fashionable point by the barber, and his cap was decked out with long floating ribbons, with a golden anchor at each end. For the moment she almost saw in him her son Pierre, who, twenty years before, had also been a sailor in the navy, and the remembrance of the far past, with all its dead, stealthily shadowed the present hour.

But the sadness soon passed away. Arm-in-arm they strolled on, happy to be together; and it was then that the others had pretended to see in her his sweetheart, and voted her "a trifle old."

She had taken him, for a treat, to dine in an inn kept by some people from Paimpol, which had been recommended to her as rather cheap. And then, still arm-in-arm, they had sauntered through Brest, looking at the shop-windows. There never were such funny stories told as those she told her grandson to make him laugh; of course all in Paimpol Breton, so that the passers-by might not understand.

CHAPTER VIII—OLD AND YOUNG

She stayed three days with him, three happy days, though over them hung a dark and ominous forecast; one might as well call them three days of respite.

At last she was forced to return to Ploubazlanec, for she had come to the end of her little savings, and Sylvestre was to embark the day afterward. The sailors are always inexorably kept in barracks the day before foreign cruises (a custom that seems rather barbarous at first, but which is a necessary precaution against the "flings" they would have before leaving definitely).

Oh that last day! She had done her very best to hatch up some more funny stories in her head, to tell her boy just at the parting; but she had remembered nothing—no; only tears had welled up, and at every moment sobs choked her. Hanging on his arm, she reminded him of a thousand things he was not to forget to do, and he also tried hard to repress his tears. They had ended by going into a church to say their prayers together.

It was by the night train that she went. To save a few pence, they had gone on foot to the station; he carrying her box, and holding her on his strong arm, upon which she weighed heavily.

She was so very, very tired—poor old lady! She had scarcely any strength left after the exertion of the last three or four days. Her shoulders were bent under her brown shawl, and she had no force to bear herself up; her youngish look was gone, and she felt the weight of her seventy-six years.

Oh! how her heart ached at the thought that it was all over, and that in a few moments she must leave him! Was he really to go out so far, to

China, perhaps to slaughter. She still had him there with her, quite close, her poor hands could yet grasp him—and yet he must go; all the strength of her will, all her tears, and all her great heartrending despair—all! would nothing be of avail to keep him back?

With her ticket, and her lunch-basket, and her mittens in her grasp, agitated, she gave him her last blessing and advice, and he answered her with an obedient "Ay, ay," bending his head tenderly towards her and gazing lovingly at her, in his soft childish way.

"Now then, old lady, you must make up your mind plaguey quick if you want to go by this train!"

The engine whistled. Suddenly terrified at the idea of losing the train, she bore her box from Sylvestre's grasp, and flinging it down, threw her arms round his neck in a last and supreme embrace.

Many people on the platform stared at them, but not one smiled. Hustled about by the porters, worn out and full of pain, she pressed into the first carriage near; the door was banged quickly upon her, while Sylvestre, with all the speed of a young sailor, rushed out of the station to the rails beside the line to see the train pass.

A shrill screeching whistle, a noisy grinding of the wheels, and his grandmother passed away, leaving him leaning against the gate and swinging up his cap with its flying ribbons, while she, hanging out of the window of her third-class carriage, made an answering signal with her handkerchief; and for as long as she could see the dark blue-clad figure, that was her child, followed him with her eyes, throwing her whole soul into that "good-bye!" kept back to the last, and always uncertain of realization when sailors are concerned.

Look long at your little Sylvestre, poor old woman; until the very latest moment, do not lose sight of his fleeting shadow, which is fading away for ever.

When she could see him no longer, she fell back, completely crushing her still clean unrumpled cap, weeping and sobbing in the agony of death itself.

He had turned away slowly, with his head bent, and big tears falling down his cheeks. The autumn night had closed in; everywhere the gas was flaring, and the sailors' riotous feasts had begun anew. Paying no heed to anything about him, he passed through Brest and over the Recouvrance Bridge, to the barracks.

"Whist! here, you darling boy!" called out some nocturnal prowlers to him; but he passed on, and entering the barracks, flung himself down in his hammock, weeping, all alone, and hardly sleeping until dawn.

CHAPTER IX—THE EASTERN VOYAGE

Sylvestre was soon out on the ocean, rapidly whisked away over the unknown seas, far more blue than Iceland's. The ship that carried him off to the confines of Asia was ordered to go at full speed and stop nowhere. Ere long he felt that he was far away, for the speed was unceasing, and even without a care for the sea or the wind. As he was a topman, he lived perched aloft, like a bird, avoiding the soldiers crowded upon the deck.

Twice they stopped, however, on the coast of Tunis, to take up more Zouaves and mules; from afar he had perceived the white cities amid sands and arid hills. He had even come down from his top to look at the dark-brown men draped in their white robes who came off in small boats to peddle fruit; his mates told him that these were Bedouins.

The heat and the sun, which were unlessened by the autumn season, made him feel out of his element.

One day they touched at Port Said. All the flags of Europe waved overhead from long staves, which gave it an aspect of Babel on a feast-day, and the glistening sands surrounded the town like a moving sea.

They had stopped there, touching the quays, almost in the midst of the long streets full of wooden shanties. Since his departure, Sylvestre never had seen the outside world so closely, and the movement and numbers of boats excited and amused him.

With never-ending screeching from their escape-pipes, all these boats crowded up in the long canal, as narrow as a ditch, which wound itself in a silvery line through the infinite sands. From his post on high he could see them as in a procession under a window, till disappearing in the plain.

On the canal all kinds of costumes could be seen; men in many-coloured attire, busy and shouting like thunder. And at night the clamour of confused bands of music mingled with the diabolical screams of the locomotives, playing noisy tunes, as if to drown the heart-breaking sorrow of the exiles who for ever passed onward.

The next day, at sunrise, they, too, glided into the narrow ribbon of water between the sands. For two days the steaming in the long file through the desert lasted, then another sea opened before them, and they were once again upon the open. They still ran at full speed through this warmer expanse, stained like red marble, with their boiling wake like blood. Sylvestre remained all the time up in his top, where he would hum his old song of "Jean-Francois de Nantes," to remind him of his dear brother Yann, of Iceland, and the good old bygone days.

Sometimes, in the depths of the shadowy distance, some wonderfully tinted mountain would arise. Notwithstanding the distance and the dimness around, the names of those projected capes of countries appeared as the eternal landmarks on the great roadways of the earth to the steersmen of this vessel; but a topman is carried on like an inanimate thing, knowing nothing, and unconscious of the distance over the everlasting, endless waves.

All he felt was a terrible estrangement from the things of this world, which grew greater and greater; and the feeling was very defined and exact as he looked upon the seething foam behind, and tried to remember how long had lasted this pace that never slackened night or day. Down on deck, the crowd of men, huddled together in the shadow of the awnings, panted with weariness. The water and the air, even the very light above, had a dull, crushing splendour; and the fadeless glory of those elements were as a very mockery of the human beings whose physical lives are so ephemeral.

Once, up in his crow's nest, he was gladdened by the sight of flocks of tiny birds, of an unknown species, which fell upon the ship like a whirlwind of coal dust. They allowed themselves to be taken and stroked, being worn out with fatigue. All the sailors had them as pets upon their shoulders. But soon the most exhausted among them began to die, and before long they died by thousands on the rigging, yards, ports, and sails—poor little things!—under the blasting sun of the Red Sea. They had come to destruction, off the Great Desert, fleeing before a sandstorm. And through fear of falling into the blue waters that stretched on all sides, they had ended their last feeble flight upon the passing ship. Over yonder, in some distant region of Libya, they had been fledged in masses. Indeed, there were so many of them, that their blind and unkind mother, Nature, had driven away before her this surplus, as unmoved as if they had been superabundant men. On the scorching funnels and ironwork of the ship they died away; the deck was strewn with their puny forms, only yesterday so full of life, songs, and love. Now, poor little black dots, Sylvestre and the others picked them up, spreading out their delicate blue wings, with a look of pity, and swept them overboard into the abysmal sea.

Next came hosts of locusts, the spawn of those conjured up by Moses, and the ship was covered with them. At length, though, it surged on a lifeless blue sea, where they saw no things around them, except from time to time the flying fish skimming along the level water.

CHAPTER X—THE ORIENT

Rain in torrents, under a heavy black sky. This was India. Sylvestre had just set foot upon land, chance selecting him to complete the crew of a whale boat. He felt the warm shower upon him through the thick foliage, and looked around, surprised at the novel sight. All was magnificently green; the leaves of the trees waved like gigantic feathers, and the people walking beneath them had large velvety eyes, which seemed to close under the weight of their lashes. The very wind that brought the rain had the odour of musk and flowers.

At a distance, dusky girls beckoned him to come to them. Some happy strain they sang, like the "Whist! here, you darling boy!" so often heard at Brest. But seductive as was their country, their call was imperious and exasperating, making his very flesh shudder. Their perfect bosoms rose and fell under transparent muslin, in which they were solely draped; they were glowing and polished as in bronze statues. Hesitating, fascinated by them, he wavered about, following them; but the boatswain's sharp shrill whistle rent the air with bird-like trills, summoning him hurriedly back to his boat, about to push off.

He took his flight, and bade farewell to India's beauties.

After a second week of the blue sea, they paused off another land of dewy verdure. A crowd of yellow men appeared, yelling out and pressing on deck, bringing coal in baskets.

"Already in China?" asked Sylvestre, at the sight of those grotesque figures in pigtails.

"Bless you, no, not yet," they told him; "have a little more patience."

It was only Singapore. He went up into his mast-top again, to avoid the black dust tossed about by the breeze, while the coal was feverishly heaped up in the bunkers from little baskets.

One day, at length, they arrived off a land called Tourane, where the *Circe* was anchored, to blockade the port. This was the ship to which Sylvestre had been long ago assigned, and he was left there with his bag.

On board he met with two mates from home, Icelanders, who were captains of guns for the time being. Through the long, hot, still evenings, when there was no work to be done, they clustered on deck apart from the others, to form together a little Brittany of remembrances.

Five months he passed there in inaction and exile, locked up in the cheerless bay, with the feverish desire to go out and fight and slay, for change's sake.

CHAPTER XI—A CURIOUS RENCONTRE

In Paimpol again, on the last day of February, before the setting-out for Iceland. Gaud was standing up against her room door, pale and still. For Yann was below, chatting to her father. She had seen him come in, and indistinctly heard his voice.

All through the winter they never had met, as if some invincible fate always had kept them apart.

After the failure to find him in her walk to Pors-Even, she had placed some hope on the *Pardon des Islandais* where there would be many chances for them to see and talk to one another, in the market-place at dusk, among the crowd.

But on the very morning of the holiday, though the streets were already draped in white and strewn with green garlands, a hard rain had fallen in torrents, brought from the west by a soughing wind; never had so black a sky shadowed Paimpol. "What a pity! the boys won't come over from Ploubazlanec now," had moaned the lasses, whose sweethearts dwelt there. And they did not come, or else had gone straight into the taverns to drink together.

There had been no processions or strolls, and she, with her heart aching more than ever, had remained at her window the whole evening listening to the water streaming over the roofs, and the fishers' noisy songs rising and falling out of the depths of the taverns.

For the last few days she had been expecting this visit, surmising truly that old Gaos would send his son to terminate the business concerning the sale of the boat, as he did not care to come into Paimpol himself. She determined then that she would go straight to him, and, unlike other girls, speak out frankly, to have her conscience clear on the subject. She would reproach him with having sought her out and having abandoned her like a man without honour. If it were only stubbornness, timidity, his great love for his sailor-life, or simply the fear of a refusal, as Sylvestre had hinted, why, all these objections would disappear, after a frank, fair understanding between them. His fond smile might return, which had charmed and won her the winter before, and all would be settled. This hope gave her strength and courage, and sweetened her impatience. From afar, things always appear so easy and simple to say and to do.

This visit of Yann's fell by chance at a convenient hour. She was sure that her father, who was sitting and smoking, would not get up to walk part of the way with him; so in the empty passage she might have her explanation out with him.

But now that the time had come, such boldness seemed extreme. The bare idea of looking him face to face at the foot of those stairs, made her tremble; and her heart beat as if it would break. At any moment the door below might open, with the squeak she knew so well, to let him out!

"No, no, she never would dare; rather would she die of longing and sorrow, than attempt such an act." She already made a few return steps towards the back of her room, to regain her seat and work. But she stopped again, hesitating and afraid, remembering that to-morrow was the sailing day for Iceland, and that this occasion stood alone. If she let it slip by, she would have to wait through months upon months of solitude and despair, languishing for his return—losing another whole summer of her life.

Below, the door opened—Yann was coming out!

Suddenly resolute, she rushed downstairs, and tremblingly stood before him.

"Monsieur Yann, I—I wish to speak to you, please."

"To me, Mademoiselle Gaud?" queried he, lowering his voice and snatching off his hat.

He looked at her fiercely, with a hard expression in his flashing eyes, and his head thrown back, seeming even to wonder if he ought to stop for her at all. With one foot ready to start away, he stood straight up against the wall, as if to be as far apart from her as possible, in the narrow passage, where he felt imprisoned.

Paralyzed, she could remember nothing of what she had wished to say; she had not thought he would try and pass on without listening to her. What an affront!

"Does our house frighten you, Monsieur Yann?" she asked, in a dry, odd tone—not at all the one she wished to use.

He turned his eyes away, looking outside; his cheeks blazed red, a rush of blood burned all his face, and his quivering nostrils dilated with every breath, keeping time with the heavings of his chest, like a young bull's.

"The night of the ball," she tried to continue, "when we were together, you bade me good-bye, not as a man speaks to an indifferent person. Monsieur Yann, have you no memory? What have I done to vex you?"

The nasty western breeze blowing in from the street ruffled his hair and the frills of Gaud's *coiffe*, and behind them a door was banged furiously. The passage was not meet for talking of serious matters in. After these first phrases, choking, Gaud remained speechless, feeling her head spin, and without ideas. They still advanced towards the street door; he seemed so anxious to get away, and she was so determined not to be shaken off.

Outside the wind blew noisily and the sky was black. A sad livid light fell upon their faces through the open door. And an opposite neighbour looked at them: what could the pair be saying to one another in that passage together, looking so troubled? What was wrong over at the Mevel's?

"Nay, Mademoiselle Gaud," he answered at last, turning away with the powerful grace of a young lion, "I've heard folks talk about us quite enough already! Nay, Mademoiselle Gaud, for, you see, you are rich, and we are not people of the same class. I am not the fellow to come after a 'swell' lady."

He went forth on his way. So now all was over for ever and ever. She had not even said what she wished in that interview, which had only made her seem a very bold girl in his sight. What kind of a fellow was this Yann, with his contempt for women, his scorn for money, and all desirable things?

At first she remained fixed to the spot, sick with giddiness, as things swam around her. One intolerably painful thought suddenly struck her like a flash of lightning—Yann's comrades, the Icelanders, were waiting for him below in the market-place. What if he were to tell them this as a good joke—what a still more odious affront upon her! She quickly returned to her room to watch them through her window-curtains.

Before the house, indeed, she saw the men assembled, but they were simply contemplating the weather, which was becoming worse and worse, and discussed the threatening rain.

"It'll only be a shower. Let's go in and drink away the time, till it passes."

They poked jokes and laughed loudly over Jeannie Caroff and other beauties; but not even one of them looked up at *her* window. They were all joyful, except Yann, who said nothing, and remained grave and sad. He did not go in to drink with them; and without noticing either them or the rain, which had begun to fall, he slowly walked away under the shower, as if absorbed in his thoughts, crossing the market-place towards Ploubazlanec.

Then she forgave him all, and a feeling of hopeless tenderness for him came, instead of the bitter disappointment that previously had filled her heart. She sat down and held her head between her hands. What could she do now?

Oh! if he had listened only a moment to her, or if he could come into that room, where they might speak together alone, perhaps all might yet be arranged. She loved him enough to tell him so to his face. She would say to him: "You sought me out when I asked you for nothing; now I am yours with my whole soul, if you will have me. I don't mind a bit being the wife of a fisherman, and yet, if I liked, I need but choose among all the young men of Paimpol; but I do love you, because, notwithstanding all, I believe you to be better than others. I'm tolerably well-to-do, and I know I am pretty; although I have lived in towns, I am sure that I am not a spoiled girl, as I never have done anything wrong; then, if I love you so, why shouldn't you take me?"

But all this never would be said except in dreams; it was too late! Yann would not hear her. Try and talk to him a second time? Oh, no! what kind of a creature would he take her then to be? She would rather die.

Yet to-morrow they would all start for Iceland. The whitish February daylight streamed into her fine room. Chill and lonely she fell upon one of the chairs along the wall. It seemed to her as if the whole world were crashing and falling in around her. All things past and present were as if buried in a fearful abyss, which yawned on all sides of her. She wished her life would end, and that she were lying calm beneath some cold tombstone, where no more pain might touch her.

But she had sincerely forgiven him, and no hatred mingled with her desperate love.

CHAPTER XII—STRIKING THE ROCK UNKNOWN

The sea, the gray sea once more, where Yann was gently gliding along its broad, trackless road, that leads the fishermen every year to the Land of Ice.

The day before, when they all had set off to the music of the old hymns, there blew a brisk breeze from the south, and all the ships with their outspread sails had dispersed like so many gulls; but that breeze had suddenly subsided, and speed had diminished; great fog-banks covered the watery surface.

Yann was perhaps quieter than usual. He said that the weather was too calm, and appeared to excite himself, as if he would drive away some care that weighed upon him. But he had nothing to do but be carried serenely in the midst of serene things; only to breathe and let himself live. On looking out, only the deep gray masses around could be seen; on listening, only silence.

Suddenly there was an almost imperceptible rumbling, which came from below, accompanied by a grinding sensation, as when a brake comes hard down on carriage wheels. The *Marie* ceased all movement. They had struck. Where, and on what? Some bank off the English coast probably. For since overnight they had been able to see nothing, with those curtains of mist.

The men ran and rushed about, their bustle contrasting strongly with the sudden rigidity of their ship. How had the *Marie* come to a stop in that spot? In the midst of that immensity of fluid in this dull weather, seeming to be almost without consistence, she had been seized by some resistless immovable power hidden beneath the waves; she was tight in its grasp, and might perish there.

Who has not seen poor birds caught by their feet in the lime? At first they can scarcely believe they are caught; it changes nothing in their aspect; but they soon are sure that they are held fast, and in danger of never getting free again. And when they struggle to get free, and the sticky stuff soils their wings and heads, they gradually assume that pitiful look of a dumb creature in distress, about to die. Such was the case with the *Marie*. At first it did not seem much to be concerned about; she certainly was careened a little on one side, but it was broad morning, and the weather was fair and calm; one had to know such things by experience to become uneasy, and understand that it was a serious matter.

The captain was to be pitied. It was his fault, as he had not understood exactly where they were. He wrung his hands, saying: "God help us! God help us!" in a voice of despair.

Close to them, during a lifting of the fog, they could distinguish a headland, but not recognize it. But the mists covered it anew, and they saw it no longer.

There was no sail or smoke in sight. They all jostled about, hurrying and knocking the deck lumber over. Their dog Turc, who did not usually mind the movement of the sea, was greatly affected too by this incident, these sounds from down below, these heavy wallowings when the low swell passed under, and the sudden calm that afterwards followed; he understood that all this was unusual, and hid himself away in corners, with his tail between his legs. They got out the boats to carry the kedges and set them firm, and tried to row her out of it by uniting all their forces together upon the tow-lines—a heavy piece of work this, which lasted ten successive hours. So, when evening came, the poor bark, which had only that morning been so fresh and light, looked almost swamped, fouled, and good for nothing. She had fought hard, floundered about on all sides, but still remained there, fixed as in a dock.

Night was overtaking them; the wind and the waves were rising; things were growing worse, when, all of a sudden, towards six o'clock, they were let go clear, and could be off again, tearing asunder the tow-lines, which they had left to keep her head steady. The men wept, rushing about like madmen, cheering from stem to stern—"We're afloat, boys!"

They were afloat, with a joy that cannot be described; what it was to feel themselves going forwards on a buoyant craft again, instead of on the semi-wreck it was before, none but a seaman feels, and few of them can tell.

Yann's sadness had disappeared too. Like his ship, he became lively once more, cured by the healthy manual labour; he had found his reckless look again, and had thrown off his glum thoughts.

Next morning, when the kedges were fished up, the *Marie* went on her way to Iceland, and Yann's heart, to all appearance, was as free as in his early years.

CHAPTER XIII—HOME NEWS

The home letters were being distributed on board the *Circe*, at anchor at Ha-Long, over on the other side of the earth. In the midst of a group of sailors, the purser called out, in a loud voice, the names of the fortunate men who had letters to receive. This went on at evening, on the ship's side, all crushing round a funnel.

"Moan, Sylvestre!" There was one for him, postmarked "Paimpol," but it was not Gaud's writing. What did that mean? from whom did it come else?

After having turned and flourished it about, he opened it fearingly, and read:

"PLOUBAZLANEC, March 5th, 1884.

"MY DEAR GRANDSON:"

So, it was from his dear old granny. He breathed free again. At the bottom of the letter she even had placed her signature, learned by heart, but trembling like a school-girl's scribble: "Widow Moan."

"Widow Moan!" With a quick spontaneous movement he carried the paper to his lips and kissed the poor name, as a sacred relic. For this letter arrived at a critical moment of his life; to-morrow at dawn, he was to set out for the battlefield.

It was in the middle of April; Bac-Ninh and Hong-Hoa had just been taken. There was no great warfare going on in Tonquin, yet the reinforcements arriving were not sufficient; sailors were taken from all the ships to make up the deficit in the corps already disembarked. Sylvestre, who had languished so long in the midst of cruises and blockades, had just been selected with some others to fill up the vacancies.

It is true that now peace was spoken of, but something told them that they yet would disembarck in good time to fight a bit. They packed their bags, made all their other preparations, and said good-bye, and all the evening through they strolled about with their unfortunate mates who had to remain, feeling much grander and prouder than they. Each in his own way showed his impression at this departure—some were grave and serious, others exuberant and talkative.

Sylvestre was very quiet and thoughtful, though impatient; only, when they looked at him, his smile seemed to say, "Yes, I'm one of the fighting party, and huzza! the action is for to-morrow morning!"

Of gunshots and battle he formed but an incomplete idea as yet; but they fascinated him, for he came of a valiant race.

The strange writing of his letter made him anxious about Gaud, and he drew near a porthole to read the epistle through. It was difficult amid all those half-naked men pressing round, in the unbearable heat of the gundeck.

As he thought she would do, in the beginning of her letter Granny Moan explained why she had had to take recourse to the inexperienced hand of an old neighbour:

"My dear child, I don't ask your cousin to write for me to-day, as she is in great trouble. Her father died suddenly two days ago. It appears that his whole fortune has been lost through unlucky gambling last winter in Paris. So his house and furniture will have to be sold. Nobody in the place was expecting this. I think, dear child, that this will pain you as much as it does me.

"Gaos, the son, sends you his kind remembrance; he has renewed his articles with Captain Guermeur of the *Marie*, and the departure for Iceland was rather early this year, for they set sail on the first of the month, two days before our poor Gaud's trouble, and he don't know of it yet.

"But you can easily imagine that we shall not get them wed now, for she will be obliged to work for her daily bread."

Sylvestre dwelt stupor-stricken; this bad news quite spoiled his glee at going out to fight.

PART III — IN THE SHADOW

CHAPTER I—THE SKIRMISH

Hark! a bullet hurtles through the air!

Sylvestre stops short to listen!

He is upon an infinite meadow, green with the soft velvet carpet of spring. The sky is gray, lowering, as if to weigh upon one's very shoulders.

They are six sailors reconnoitring among the fresh rice-fields, in a muddy pathway.

Hist! again the whizz, breaking the silence of the air—a shrill, continuous sound, a kind of prolonged *zing*, giving one a strong impression that the pellets buzzing by might have stung fatally.

For the first time in his life Sylvestre hears that music. The bullets coming towards a man have a different sound from those fired by himself: the far-off report is attenuated, or not heard at all, so it is easier to distinguish the sharp rush of metal as it swiftly passes by, almost grazing one's ears.

Crack! whizz! ping! again and yet again! The balls fall in regular showers now. Close by the sailors they stop short, and are buried in the flooded soil of the rice-fields, accompanied by a faint splash, like hail falling sharp and swift in a puddle of water.

The marines looked at one another as if it was all a piece of odd fun, and said:

"Only John Chinaman! pish!"

To the sailors, Annamites, Tonquinese, or "Black Flags" are all of the same Chinese family. It is difficult to show their contempt and mocking rancour, as well as eagerness for "bowling over the beggars," when they speak of "the Chinese."

Two or three bullets are still flying about, more closely grazing; they can be seen bouncing like grasshoppers in the green. The slight shower of lead did not last long.

Perfect silence returns to the broad verdant plain, and nowhere can anything be seen moving. The same six are still there, standing on the watch, scenting the breeze, and trying to discover whence the volley came. Surely from over yonder, by that clump of bamboos, which looks like an island of feathers in the plain; behind it several pointed roofs appear half hidden. So they all made for it, their feet slipping or sinking into the soaked soil. Sylvestre runs foremost, on his longer, more nimble legs.

No more buzz of bullets; they might have thought they were dreaming.

As in all the countries of the world, some features are the same; the cloudy gray skies and the fresh tints of fields in spring-time, for example; one could imagine this upon French meadows, and these young fellows, running merrily over them, playing a very different sport from this game of death.

But as they approach, the bamboos show the exotic delicacy of their foliage, and the village roofs grow sharper in the singularity of their curves, and yellow men hidden behind advance to reconnoitre; their flat faces are contracted by fear and spitefulness. Then suddenly they rush out screaming, and deploy into a long line, trembling, but decided and dangerous.

"The Chinese!" shout the sailors again, with their same brave smile.

But this time they find that there are a good many—too many; and one of them turning round perceives other Chinese coming from behind, springing up from the long tall grass.

At this moment, young Sylvestre came out grand; his old granny would have been proud to see him such a warrior. Since the last few days he had altered. His face was bronzed, and his voice strengthened. He was in his own element here.

In a moment of supreme indecision the sailors hit by the bullets almost yielded to an impulse of retreat, which would certainly have been death to them all; but Sylvestre continued to advance, clubbing his rifle, and fighting a whole band, knocking them down right and left with smashing blows from the butt-end. Thanks to him the situation was reversed; that panic or madness that blindly deceives all in these leaderless skirmishes had now passed over to the Chinese side, and it was they who began to retreat.

It was soon all over; they were fairly taking to their heels. The six sailors, reloading their repeating rifles, shot them down easily; upon the grass lay dead bodies by red pools, and skulls were emptying their brains into the river.

They fled, cowering like leopards. Sylvestre ran after them, although he had two wounds—a lance-thrust in the thigh and a deep gash in his arm; but feeling nothing save the intoxication of battle, that unreasoning fever that comes of vigorous blood, gives lofty courage to simple souls, and made the heroes of antiquity.

One whom he was pursuing turned round, and with a spasm of desperate terror took a deliberate aim at him. Sylvestre stopped short, smiling scornfully, sublime, to let him fire, and seeing the direction of the aim, only shifted a little to the left. But with the pressure upon the trigger the barrel of the Chinese jingal deviated slightly in the same direction. He suddenly felt a smart rap upon his breast, and in a flash of thought understood what it was, even before feeling any pain; he turned towards the others following, and tried to cry out to them the traditional phrase of the old soldier, "I think it's all up with me!" In the great breath that he inhaled after having run, to refill his lungs with air, he felt the air rush in also by a hole in his right breast, with a horrible gurgling, like the blast in a broken bellows. In that same time his mouth filled with blood, and a sharp pain shot through his side, which rapidly grew worse, until it became atrocious and unspeakable. He whirled round two or three times, his brain swimming too; and gasping for breath through the rising red tide that choked him, fell heavily in the mud.

CHAPTER II—"OUT, BRIEF CANDLE!"

About a fortnight later, as the sky was darkening at the approach of the rains, and the heat more heavily weighed over yellow Tonquin, Sylvestre brought to Hanoi, was sent to Ha-Long, and placed on board a hospital-ship about to return to France.

He had been carried about for some time on different stretchers, with intervals of rest at the ambulances. They had done all they could for him; but under the insufficient conditions, his chest had filled with water on the pierced side, and the gurgling air entered through the wound, which would not close up.

He had received the military medal, which gave him a moment's joy. But he was no longer the warrior of old—resolute of gait, and steady in his resounding voice. All that had vanished before the long-suffering and weakening fever. He had become a home-sick boy again; he hardly spoke except in answering occasional questions, in a feeble and almost inaudible voice. To feel oneself so sick and so far away; to think that it wanted so many days before he could reach home! Would he ever live until then, with his strength ebbing away? Such a terrifying feeling of distance continually haunted him and weighed at every wakening; and when, after a few hours' stupor, he awoke from the sickening pain of his wounds, with feverish heat and the whistling sound in his pierced bosom, he implored them to put him on board, in spite of everything. He was very heavy to carry into his ward, and without intending it, they gave him some cruel jolts on the way.

They laid him on one of the iron camp bedsteads placed in rows, hospital fashion, and then he set out in an inverse direction, on his long journey through the seas. Instead of living like a bird in the full wind of the tops, he remained below deck, in the midst of the bad air of medicines, wounds, and misery.

During the first days the joy of being homeward bound made him feel a little better. He could even bear being propped up in bed with pillows, and at times he asked for his box. His seaman's chest was a deal box, bought in Paimpol, to keep all his loved treasures in; inside were letters from Granny Yvonne, and also from Yann and Gaud, a copy-book into which he had copied some sea-songs, and one of the works of Confucius in Chinese, caught up at random during pillage; on the blank sides of its leaves he had written the simple account of his campaign.

Nevertheless he got no better, and after the first week, the doctors decided that death was imminent. They were near the Line now, in the stifling heat of storms. The troop-ship kept on her course, shaking her beds, the wounded and the dying; quicker and quicker she sped over the tossing sea, troubled still as during the sway of the monsoons.

Since leaving Ha-Long more than one patient died, and was consigned to the deep water on the high road to France; many of the narrow beds no longer bore their suffering burdens.

Upon this particular day it was very gloomy in the travelling hospital; on account of the high seas it had been necessary to close the iron port-lids, which made the stifling sick-room more unbearable. Sylvestre was worse; the end was nigh. Lying always upon his wounded side, he pressed upon it with both hands with all his remaining strength, to try and allay the watery decomposition that rose in his right lung, and to breathe with the other lung only. But by degrees the other was affected and the ultimate agony had begun.

Dreams and visions of home haunted his brain; in the hot darkness, beloved or horrible faces bent over him; he was in a never-ending hallucination, through which floated apparitions of Brittany and Iceland. In the morning was called in the priest, and the old man, who was used to seeing sailors die, was astonished to find so pure a soul in so strong and manly a body.

He cried out for air, air! but there was none anywhere; the ventilators no long gave any; the attendant, who was fanning him with a Chinese fan, only moved unhealthy vapours over him of sickening staleness, which revolted all lungs. Sometimes fierce, desperate fits came over him; he wished to tear himself away from that bed, where he felt death would come to seize him, and rush above into the full fresh wind and try to live again. Oh! to be like those others, scrambling about among the rigging, and living among the masts. But his extreme effort only ended in the feeble lifting of his weakened head; something like the incompleted movement of a sleeper. He could not manage it, but fell back in the hollow of his crumpled bed, partly chained there by death; and each time, after the fatigue of a like shock, he lost all consciousness.

To please him they opened a port at last, although it was dangerous, the sea being very rough. It was going on for six in the evening. When the disk was swung back, a red light entered, glorious and radiant. The dying sun appeared upon the horizon in dazzling splendour, through a torn rift in a gloomy sky; its blinding light glanced over the waves, and lit up the floating hospital, like a waving torch.

But no air rushed in; the little there was outside, was powerless to enter and drive before it the fevered atmosphere. Over all sides of that boundless equatorial sea, floated a warm and heavy moisture, unfit for respiration. No air on any side, not even for the poor gasping fellows on their deathbeds.

One vision disturbed him greatly; it was of his old grandmother, walking quickly along a road, with a heartrending look of alarm; from low-lying funereal clouds above her, fell the drizzling rain; she was on her way to Paimpol, summoned thither to be informed of his death.

He was struggling now, with the death-rattle in his throat. From the corners of his mouth they sponged away the water and blood, which had welled up in quantities from his chest in writhing agony. Still the grand, glorious sun lit up all, like a conflagration of the whole world, with blood-laden clouds; through the aperture of the port-hole, a wide streak of crimson fire blazed in, and, spreading over Sylvestre's bed, formed a halo around him.

At that very moment that same sun was to be seen in Brittany, where midday was about to strike. It was, indeed, the same sun, beheld at the precise moment of its never-ending round; but here it kept quite another hue. Higher up in the bluish sky, it kept shedding a soft white light on grandmother Yvonne, sitting out at her door, sewing.

In Iceland, too, where it was morning, it was shining at that same moment of death. Much paler there, it seemed as if it only showed its face by some miracle. Sadly it shed its rays over the fjord where *La Marie* floated; and now its sky was lit up by a pure northern light, which always gives the idea of a frozen planet's reflection, without an atmosphere. With a cold accuracy, it outlined all the essentials of that stony chaos that is Iceland; the whole of the country as seen from *La*

Marie seemed fixed in one same perspective and held upright. Yann was there, lit up by a strange light, fishing, as usual, in the midst of this lunar-like scenery.

As the beam of fiery flame that came through the port-hole faded, and the sun disappeared completely under the gilded billows, the eyes of the grandson rolled inward toward his brow as if to fall back into his head.

They closed his eyelids with their own long lashes, and Sylvestre became calm and beautiful again, like a reclining marble statue of manly repose.

CHAPTER III—THE GRAVE ABROAD

I cannot refrain from telling you about Sylvestre's funeral, which I conducted myself in Singapore. We had thrown enough other dead into the Sea of China, during the early days of the home voyage; and as the Malay land was quite near, we decided to keep his remains a few hours longer; to bury him fittingly.

It was very early in the morning, on account of the terrible sun. In the boat that carried him ashore, his corpse was shrouded in the national flag. The city was in sleep as we landed. A wagonette, sent by the French Consul, was waiting on the quay; we laid Sylvestre upon it, with a wooden cross made on board—the paint still wet upon it, for the carpenter had to hurry over it, and the white letters of his name ran into the black ground.

We crossed that Babel in the rising sun. And then it was such an emotion to find the serene calm of an European place of worship in the midst of the distasteful turmoil of the Chinese country. Under the high white arch, where I stood alone with my sailors, the "*Dies Iroe*," chanted by a missionary priest, sounded like a soft magical incantation. Through the open doors we could see sights that resembled enchanted gardens, exquisite verdure and immense palm-trees, the wind shook the large flowering shrubs and their perfumed crimson petals fell like rain, almost to the church itself. Thence we marched to the ceremony, very far off. Our little procession of sailors was very unpretentious, but the coffin remained conspicuously wrapped in the flag of France. We had to traverse the Chinese quarter, through seething crowds of yellow men; and then the Malay and Indian suburbs, where all types of Asiatic faces looked upon us with astonishment.

Then came the open country already heated; through shady groves where exquisite butterflies, on velvety blue wings, flitted in masses. On either side, waved tall luxuriant palms, and quantities of flowers in splendid profusion. At last we came to the cemetery, with mandarins' tombs and many-coloured inscriptions, adorned with paintings of dragons and other monsters; amid astounding foliage and plants growing everywhere. The spot where we laid him down to rest resembled a nook in the gardens of Indra. Into the earth we drove the little wooden cross, lettered:

SYLVESTRE MOAN, AGED 19.

And we left him, forced to go because of the hot rising sun; we turned back once more to look at him under those marvellous trees and huge nodding flowers.

CHAPTER IV—TO THE SURVIVORS, THE SPOILS

The trooper continued its course through the Indian Ocean. Down below in the floating hospital other death-scenes went on. On deck there was carelessness of health and youth. Round about, over the sea, was a very feast of pure sun and air.

In this fine trade-wind weather, the sailors, stretched in the shade of the sails, were playing with little pet parrots and making them run races. In this Singapore, which they had just left, the sailors buy all kinds of tame animals. They had all chosen baby parrots, with childish looks upon their hooknose faces; they had no tails yet; they were green, of a wonderful shade. As they went running over the clean white planks, they looked like fresh young leaves, fallen from tropical trees.

Sometimes the sailors gathered them all together in one lot, when they inspected one another funnily; twisting about their throats, to be seen under all aspects. They comically waddled about like so many lame people, or suddenly started off in a great hurry for some unknown destination; and some fell down in their excitement. And there were monkeys, learning tricks of all kinds, another source of amusement. Some were most tenderly loved and even kissed extravagantly, as they nestled against the callous bosoms of their masters, gazing fondly at them with womanish eyes, half-grotesque and half-touching.

Upon the stroke of three o'clock, the quartermasters brought on deck two canvas bags, sealed with huge red seals, bearing Sylvestre's name; for by order of the regulations in regard to the dead, all his clothes and personal worldly belongings were to be sold by auction. The sailors gaily grouped themselves around the pile; for, on board a hospital ship, too many of these sales of effects are seen to excite any particular emotion. Besides, Sylvestre had been but little known upon that ship.

His jackets and shirts and blue-striped jerseys were fingered and turned over and then bought up at different prices, the buyers forcing the bidding just to amuse themselves.

Then came the turn of the small treasure-box, which was sold for fifty sous. The letters and military medal had been taken out of it, to be sent back to the family; but not the book of songs and the work of Confucious, with the needles, cotton, and buttons, and all the petty requisites placed there by the forethought of Granny Moan for sewing and mending.

Then the quartermaster who held up the things to be sold drew out two small buddhas, taken in some pagoda to give to Gaud, and so funny were they that they were greeted with a general burst of laughter, when they appeared as the last lot. But the sailors laughed, not for want of heart, but only through thoughtlessness.

To conclude, the bags were sold, and the buyer immediately struck out the name on them to substitute his own.

A careful sweep of the broom was afterward given to clear the scrupulously clean deck of the dust and odds and ends, while the sailors returned merrily to play with their parrots and monkeys.

CHAPTER V—THE DEATH-BLOW

One day, in the first fortnight of June, as old Yvonne was returning home, some neighbours told her that she had been sent for by the Commissioner from the Naval Registry Office. Of course it concerned her grandson, but that did not frighten her in the least. The families of seafarers are used to the Naval Registry, and she, the daughter, wife, mother, and grandmother of seamen, had known that office for the past sixty years.

Doubtless it had to do with his "delegation"; or perhaps there was a small prize-money account from *La Circe* to take through her proxy. As she knew what respect was due to "*Monsieur le Commissaire*," she put on her best gown and a clean white cap, and set out about two o'clock.

Trotting along swiftly on the pathways of the cliff, she neared Paimpol; and musing upon these two months without letters, she grew a bit anxious.

She met her old sweetheart sitting out at his door. He had greatly aged since the appearance of the winter cold.

"Eh, eh! When you're ready, you know, don't make any ceremony, my beauty!" That "suit of deal" still haunted his mind.

The joyous brightness of June smiled around her. On the rocky heights there still grew the stunted reeds with their yellow blossoms; but passing into the hollow nooks sheltered against the bitter sea winds, one met with high sweet-smelling grass. But the poor old woman did not see all this, over whose head so many rapid seasons had passed, which now seemed as short as days.

Around the crumbling hamlet with its gloomy walls grew roses, pinks, and stocks; and even up on the tops of the whitewashed and mossy roofs, sprang the flowerets that attracted the first "miller" butterflies of the season.

This spring-time was almost without love in the land of Icelanders, and the beautiful lasses of proud race, who sat out dreaming on their doorsteps, seemed to look far beyond the visible things with their blue or brown eyes. The young men, who were the objects of their melancholy and desires, were remote, fishing on the northern seas.

But it was a spring-time for all that—warm, sweet, and troubling, with its buzzing of flies and perfume of young plants.

And all this soulless freshness smiled upon the poor old grandmother, who was quickly walking along to hear of the death of her last-born grandson. She neared the awful moment when this event, which had taken place in the so distant Chinese seas, was to be told to her; she was taking that sinister walk that Sylvestre had divined at his death-hour—the sight of that had torn his last agonized tears from him; his darling old granny summoned to Paimpol to be told that he was dead! Clearly he had seen her pass along that road, running straight on, with her tiny brown shawl, her umbrella, and large head-dress. And that apparition had made him toss and writhe in fearful anguish, while the huge, red sun of the Equator, disappearing in its glory, peered through the port-hole of the hospital to watch him die. But he, in his last hallucination, had seen his old granny moving under a rain-laden sky, and on the contrary a joyous laughing spring-time mocked her on all sides.

Nearing Paimpol, she became more and more uneasy, and improved her speed. Now she is in the gray town with its narrow granite streets, where the sun falls, bidding good-day to some other old women, her contemporaries, sitting at their windows. Astonished to see her; they said: "Wherever is she going so quickly, in her Sunday gown, on a week-day?"

"Monsieur le Commissaire" of the Naval Enlistment Office was not in just then. One ugly little creature, about fifteen years old, who was his clerk, sat at his desk. As he was too puny to be a fisher, he had received some education and passed his time in that same chair, in his black linen dust-sleeves, scratching away at paper.

With a look of importance, when she had said her name, he got up to get the official documents from off a shelf.

There were a great many papers—what did it all mean? Parchments, sealed papers, a sailor's record-book, grown yellow on the sea, and over all floated an odour of death. He spread them all out before the poor old woman, who began to tremble and feel dizzy. She had just recognized two of the letters which Gaud used to write for her to her grandson, and which were now returned to her never unsealed. The same thing had happened twenty years ago at the death of her son Pierre; the letters had been sent back from China to "Monsieur le Commissaire," who had given them to her thus.

Now he was reading out in a consequential voice: "Moan, Jean-Marie-Sylvestre, registered at Paimpol, folio 213, number 2091, died on board the *Bien Hoa*, on the 14th of ——."

"What—what has happened to him, my good sir?"

"Discharged—dead," he answered.

It wasn't because this clerk was unkind, but if he spoke in that brutal way, it was through want of judgment, and from lack of intelligence in the little incomplete being.

As he saw that she did not understand that technical expression, he said in Breton:

"*Marw eo!*"

"*Marw eo!*" (He is dead.)

She repeated the words after him, in her aged tremulous voice, as a poor cracked echo would send back some indifferent phrase. So what she had partly foreseen was true; but it only made her tremble; now that it was certain, it seemed to affect her no more. To begin with, her faculty to suffer was slightly dulled by old age, especially since this last winter. Pain did not strike her immediately. Something seemed to fall upside down in her brain, and somehow or another she mixed this death up with others. She had lost so many of them before. She needed a moment to grasp that this was her very last one, her darling, the object of all her prayers, life, and waiting, and of all her thoughts, already darkened by the sombre approach of second childhood.

She felt a sort of shame at showing her despair before this little gentleman who horrified her. Was that the way to tell a grandmother of her darling's death? She remained standing before the desk, stiffened, and tearing the fringes of her brown shawl with her poor aged hands, sore and chapped with washing.

How far away she felt from home! Goodness! what a long walk back to be gone through, and steadily, too, before nearing the whitewashed hut in which she longed to shut herself up, like a wounded beast who hides in its hole to die. And so she tried not to think too much and not to understand yet, frightened above all at the long home-journey.

They gave her an order to go and take, as the heiress, the thirty francs that came from the sale of Sylvestre's bag; and then the letters, the certificates, and the box containing the military medal.

She took the whole parcel awkwardly with open fingers, unable to find pockets to put them in.

She went straight through Paimpol, looking at no one, her body bent slightly like one about to fall, with a rushing of blood in her ears; pressing and hurrying along like some poor old machine, which could not be wound up, at a great pressure, for the last time, without fear of breaking its springs.

At the third mile she went along quite bent in two and exhausted; from time to time her foot struck against the stones, giving her a painful shock up to the very head. She hurried to bury herself in her home, for fear of falling and having to be carried there.

CHAPTER VI—A CHARITABLE ASSUMPTION

"Old Yvonne's tipsy!" was the cry.

She had fallen, and the street children ran after her. It was just at the boundary of the parish of Ploubazlanec, where many houses straggle along the roadside. But she had the strength to rise and hobble along on her stick.

"Old Yvonne's tipsy!"

The bold little creatures stared her full in the face, laughing. Her *coiffe* was all awry. Some of these little ones were not really wicked, and these, when they scanned her closer and saw the senile grimace of bitter despair, turned aside, surprised and saddened, daring to say nothing more.

At home, with the door tightly closed, she gave vent to the deep scream of despair that choked her, and fell down in a corner, her head against the wall. Her cap had fallen over her eyes; she threw off roughly what formerly had been so well taken care of. Her Sunday dress was soiled, and a thin mesh of yellowish white hair strayed from beneath her cap, completing her pitiful, poverty-stricken disorder.

CHAPTER VII—THE COMFORTER

Thus did Gaud, coming in for news in the evening, find her; her hair dishevelled, her arms hanging down, and her head resting against the stone wall, with a falling jaw grinning, and the plaintive whimper of a little child; she scarcely could weep any more; these grandmothers, grown too old, have no tears left in their dried-up eyes.

"My grandson is dead!" She threw the letters, papers, and medal into her caller's lap.

Gaud quickly scanned the whole, saw the news was true, and fell on her knees to pray. The two women remained there together almost dumb, through the June gloaming, which in Brittany is long but in Iceland is never-ending. On the hearth the cricket that brings joy was chirping his shrill music.

The dim dusk entered through the narrow window into the dwelling of those Moans, who had all been devoured by the sea, and whose family was now extinguished.

At last Gaud said: "*I'll* come to you, good granny, to live with you; I'll bring my bed that they've left me, and I'll take care of you and nurse you —you shan't be all alone."

She wept, too, for her little friend Sylvestre, but in her sorrow she was led involuntarily to think of another—he who had gone back to the deep-sea fishery.

They would have to write to Yann and tell him Sylvestre was dead; it was just now that the fishers were starting. Would he, too, weep for him?

Mayhap he would, for he had loved him dearly. In the midst of her own tears, Gaud thought a great deal of him; now and again waxing wroth against the hard-hearted fellow, and then pitying him at the thought of that pain which would strike him also, and which would be as a link between them both—one way and another, her heart was full of him.

CHAPTER VIII—THE BROTHER'S GRIEF

One pale August evening, the letter that announced Yann's brother's death, at length arrived on board the *Marie*, upon the Iceland seas; it was after a day of hard work and excessive fatigue, just as they were going down to sup and to rest. With eyes heavy with sleep, he read it in their dark nook below deck, lit by the yellow beam of the small lamp; at the first moment he became stunned and giddy, like one dazed out of fair understanding. Very proud and reticent in all things concerning the feelings was Yann, and he hid the letter in his blue jersey, next his breast, without saying anything, as sailors do. But he did not feel the courage to sit down with the others to supper, and disdaining even to explain why, he threw himself into his berth and fell asleep. Soon he dreamed of Sylvestre dead, and of his funeral going by.

Towards midnight, being in that state of mind that is peculiar to seaman who are conscious of the time of day in their slumber, and quite clearly see the hour draw night when to awaken for the watch—he saw the funeral, and said to himself: "I am dreaming; luckily the mate will come and wake me up, and the vision will pass away."

But when a heavy hand was laid upon him and a voice cried out: "Tumble out, Gaos! watch, boy!" he heard the slight rustling of paper at his breast, a fine ghastly music that affirmed the fact of the death. Yes, the letter! It was true, then? The more cruel, heartrending impression deepened, and he jumped up so quickly in his sudden start, that he struck his forehead against the overhead beam. He dressed and opened the hatchway to go up mechanically and take his place in the fishing.

CHAPTER IX—WORK CURES SORROW

When Yann was on deck, he looked around him with sleep-laden eyes, over the familiar circle of the sea. That night the illimitable immensity showed itself in its most astonishingly simple aspects, in neutral tints, giving only the impression of depth. This horizon, which indicated no recognisable region of the earth, or even any geological age, must have looked so many times the same since the origin of time, that, gazing upon it, one saw nothing save the eternity of things that exist and cannot help existing.

It was not the dead of night, for a patch of light, which seemed to ooze from no particular point, dimly lit up the scene. The wind sobbed as usual its aimless wail. All was gray, a fickle gray, which faded before the fixed gaze. The sea, during its mysterious rest, hid itself under feeble tints without a name.

Above floated scattered clouds; they had assumed various shapes, for, without form, things cannot exist; in the darkness they had blended together, so as to form one single vast veiling.

But in one particular spot of the sky, low down on the waters, they seemed a dark-veined marble, the streaks clearly defined although very distant; a tender drawing, as if traced by some dreamy hand—some chance effect, not meant to be viewed for long, and indeed hastening to die away. Even that alone, in the midst of this broad grandeur, appeared to mean something; one might think that the sad, undefined thought of the nothingness around was written there; and the sight involuntarily remained fixed upon it.

Yann's dazzled eyes grew accustomed to the outside darkness, and gazed more and more steadily upon that veining in the sky; it had now taken the shape of a kneeling figure with arms outstretched. He began to look upon it as a human shadow rendered gigantic by the distance itself.

In his mind, where his indefinite dreams and primitive beliefs still lingered, the ominous shadow, crushed beneath the gloomy sky, slowly coalesced with the thought of his dead brother, as if it were a last token from him.

He was used to such strange associations of ideas, that thrive in the minds of children. But words, vague as they may be, are still too precise to express those feelings; one would need that uncertain language that comes in dreams, of which upon awakening, one retains merely enigmatical, senseless fragments.

Looking upon the cloud, he felt a deep anguish, full of unknown mystery, that froze his very soul; he understood full well now that his poor little brother would never more be seen; sorrow, which had been some time penetrating the hard, rough rind of his heart, now gushed in and brimmed it over. He beheld Sylvestre again with his soft childish eyes; at the thought of embracing him no more, a veil fell between his eyelids and his eyes, against his will; and, at first, he could not rightly understand what it was—never having wept in all his manhood. But the tears began to fall heavily and swiftly down his cheeks, and then sobs rent his deep chest.

He went on with his fishing, losing no time and speaking to no one, and his two mates, though hearing him in the deep silence, pretended not to do so, for fear of irritating him, knowing him to be so haughty and reserved.

In his opinion death was the end of it all. Out of respect he often joined in the family prayers for the dead, but he believed in no after-life of the soul. Between themselves, in their long talks, the sailors all said the same, in a blunt taken-for-granted way, as a well-known fact; but it did not stop them from believing in ghosts, having a vague fear of graveyards, and an unlimited confidence in protecting saints and images, and above all a deep respect for the consecrated earth around the churches.

So Yann himself feared to be swallowed up by the sea, as if it would annihilate him, and the thought of Sylvestre, so far away on the other side of the earth, made his sorrow more dark and desperate. With his contempt for his fellows, he had no shame or constraint in weeping, no more than if he were alone.

Around the boat the chaos grew whiter, although it was only two o'clock, and at the same time it appeared to spread farther, hollowing in a fearful manner. With that kind of rising dawn, eyes opened wider, and the awakened mind could conceive better the immensity of distance, as the boundaries of visible space receded and widened away.

The pale aurora increased, seeming to come in tiny jets with slight shocks; eternal things seemed to light up by sheer transparency, as if white-flamed lamps had slowly been raised up behind the shapeless gray clouds, and held there with mysterious care, for fear of disturbing the calm, even rest of the sea. Below the horizon that colossal white lamp was the sun, which dragged itself along without strength, before taking its leisurely ascent, which began in the dawn's eye above the ocean.

On this day, the usual rosy tints were not seen; all remained pale and mournful. On board the gray ship, Yann wept alone. The tears of the fierce elder brother, together with the melancholy of this surrounding waste, were as mourning, worn in honour of the poor, obscure, young hero, upon these seas of Iceland, where half his life had been passed.

When the full light of day appeared, Yann abruptly wiped his eyes with his sleeve and ceased weeping. That grief was over now. He seemed completely absorbed by the work of the fishery, and by the monotonous routine of substantial deeds, as if he never had thought of anything else.

The catching went on apace, and there were scant hands for the work. Around about the fishers, in the immense depths, a transformation scene was taking place. The grand opening out of the infinitude, that great wonder of the morning, had finished, and the distance seemed to diminish and close in around them. How was it that before the sea had seemed so boundless!

The horizon was quite clear now, and more space seemed necessary. The void filled in with flecks and streamers that floated above, some vague as mist, others with visibly jagged edges. They fell softly amid an utter silence, like snowy gauze, but fell on all sides together, so that below them suffocation set in swiftly; it took away the breath to see the air so thickened.

It was the first of the August fogs that was rising. In a few moments the winding-sheet became universally dense; all around the *Marie* a white damp lay under the light, and in it the mast faded and disappeared.

"Here's the cursed fog now, for sure," grumbled the men. They had long ago made the acquaintance of that compulsory companion of the second part of the fishing season; but it also announced its end and the time for returning to Brittany.

It condensed into fine, sparkling drops in their beards, and shone upon their weather-beaten faces. Looking athwart ship to one another, they appeared dim as ghosts; and by comparison, nearer objects were seen more clearly under the colourless light. They took care not to inhale the air too deeply, for a feeling of chill and wet penetrated the lungs.

But the fishing was going on briskly, so that they had no time left to chatter, and they only thought of their lines. Every moment big heavy fish were drawn in on deck, and slapped down with a smack like a whip-crack; there they wriggled about angrily, flapping their tails on the deck, scattering plenty of sea-water about, and silvery scales too, in the course of their death-struggle. The sailor who split them open with his long knife, sometimes cut his own fingers, in his haste, so that his warm blood mingled with the brine.

CHAPTER X—THE WHITE FOG

Caught in the fog, they remained ten days in succession without being able to see anything. The fishing went on handsomely the while, and with so much to do there was no time for weariness. At regular intervals one of them blew a long fog-horn, whence issued a sound like the howling of a wild beast.

Sometimes, out of the depths of white fog, another bellowing answered their call. Then a sharper watch was kept. If the blasts were approaching, all ears were turned in the direction of that unknown neighbour, whom they might perhaps never see, but whose presence was nevertheless a danger. Conjectures were made about the strange vessel; it became a subject of conversation, a sort of company for them; all longing to see her, strained their eyes in vain efforts to pierce those impalpable white shrouds.

Then the mysterious consort would depart, the bellowing of her trumpet fading away in the distance, and they would remain again in the deep hush, amid the infinity of stagnant vapour. Everything was drenched with salt water; the cold became more penetrating; each day the sun took longer to sink below the horizon; there were now real nights one or two hours long, and their gray gloaming was chilly and weird.

Every morning they heaved the lead, through fear that the *Marie* might have run too near the Icelandic coast. But all the lines on board, fastened end to end, were paid out in vain—the bottom could not be touched. So they knew that they were well out in blue water.

Life on board was rough and wholesome; the comfort in the snug strong oaken cabin below was enhanced by the impression of the piercing cold outside, when they went down to supper or for rest.

In the daytime, these men, who were as secluded as monks, spoke but little among themselves. Each held his line, remaining for hours and hours in the same immovable position. They were separated by some three yards of space, but it ended in not even seeing one another.

The calm of the fog dulled the mind. Fishing so lonely, they hummed home songs, so as not to scare the fish away. Ideas came more slowly and seldom; they seemed to expand, filling in the space of time, without leaving any vacuum. They dreamed of incoherent and mysterious things, as if in slumber, and the woof of their dreams was as airy as fog itself.

This misty month of August usually terminated the Iceland season, in a quiet, mournful way. Otherwise the full physical life was the same, filling the sailors' lungs with rustling air and hardening their already strong muscles.

Yann's usual manner had returned, as if his great grief had not continued; watchful and active, quick at his fishing work, a happy-go-lucky temper, like one who had no troubles; communicative at times, but very rarely—and always carrying his head up high, with his old indifferent, domineering look.

At supper in the rough retreat, when they were all seated at table, with their knives busy on their hot plates, he occasionally laughed out as he used to do at droll remarks of his mates. In his inner self he perhaps thought of Gaud, to whom, doubtless, Sylvestre had plighted him in his last hours; and she had become a poor girl now, alone in the world. And above all, perhaps, the mourning for his beloved brother still preyed upon his heart. But this heart of his was a virgin wilderness, difficult to explore and little known, where many things took place unrevealed on the exterior.

CHAPTER XI—THE SPECTRE SHIP

One morning, going on three o'clock, while all were dreaming quietly under their winding-sheet of fog, they heard something like a clamour of voices—voices whose tones seemed strange and unfamiliar. Those on deck looked at each other questioningly.

"Who's that talking?"

Nobody. Nobody had said anything. For that matter, the sounds had seemed to come from the outer void. Then the man who had charge of the fog-horn, but had been neglecting his duty since overnight, rushed for it, and inflating his lungs to their utmost, sounded with all his might the long bellow of alarm. It was enough to make a man of iron start, in such a silence.

As if a spectre had been evoked by that thrilling, though deep-toned roar, a huge unforeseen gray form suddenly arose very loftily and towered threateningly right beside them; masts, spars, rigging, all like a ship that had taken sudden shape in the air instantly, just as a single beam of electric light evokes phantasmagoria on the screen of a magic lantern.

Men appeared, almost close enough to touch them, leaning over the bulwarks, staring at them with eyes distended in the awakening of surprise and dread.

The *Marie's* men rushed for oars, spars, boat-hooks, anything they could lay their hands on for fenders, and held them out to shove off that grisly thing and its impending visitors. Lo! these others, terrified also, put out large beams to repel them likewise.

But there came only a very faint creaking in the topmasts, as both standing gears momentarily entangled became disentangled without the least damage; the shock, very gentle in such a calm had been almost wholly deadened; indeed, it was so feeble that it really seemed as if the other ship had no substance, that it was a mere pulp, almost without weight.

When the fright was over, the men began to laugh; they had recognised each other.

"*La Marie*, ahoy! how are ye, lads?"

"Halloa! Gaos, Laumec, Guermeur!"

The spectre ship was the *Reine-Berthe*, also of Paimpol, and so the sailors were from neighbouring villages; that thick, tall fellow with the huge, black beard, showing his teeth when he laughed, was Kerjegou, one of the Ploudaniel boys, the others were from Plounes or Plounerin.

"Why didn't you blow your fog-horn, and be blowed to you, you herd of savages?" challenged Larvoer of the *Reine-Berthe*.

"If it comes to that, why didn't you blow yours, you crew of pirates—you rank mess of toad-fish?"

"Oh, no! with us, d'ye see, the sea-law differs. *We're forbidden to make any noise!*"

He made this reply with the air of giving a dark hint, and a queer smile, which afterward came back to the memory of the men of the *Marie*, and caused them a great deal of thinking. Then, as if he thought he had said too much, he concluded with a joke:

"Our fog-horn, d'ye see, was burst by this rogue here a-blowing too hard into it." He pointed to a sailor with a face like a Triton, a man all bull-neck and chest, extravagantly broad-shouldered, low-set upon his legs, with something unspeakably grotesque and unpleasant in the deformity of strength.

While they were looking at each other, waiting for breeze or undercurrent to move one vessel faster than the other and separate them, a general palaver began. Leaning over the side, but holding each other off at a respectable distance with their long wooden props, like besieged pikemen repelling an assault, they began to chat about home, the last letters received, and sweethearts and wives.

"I say! my old woman," said Kerjegou, "tells me she's had the little boy we were looking for; that makes half-score-two now!"

Another had found himself the father of twins; and a third announced the marriage of pretty Jenny Caroff, a girl well known to all the Icelanders, with some rich and infirm old resident of the Commune of Plourivo. As they were eyeing each other as if through white gauze, this also appeared to alter the sound of the voices, which came as if muffled and from far away.

Meanwhile Yann could not take his eyes off one of those brother fishermen, a little grizzled fellow, whom he was quite sure he never had seen before, but who had, nevertheless, straightway said to him, "How d'o, long Yann?" with all the familiarity of bosom acquaintance. He wore the provoking ugliness of a monkey, with an apish twinkling of mischief too in his piercing eyes.

"As for me," said Larvoer, of the *Reine-Berthe*, "I've been told of the death of the grandson of old Yvonne Moan, of Ploubazlanec—who was serving his time in the navy, you know, in the Chinese squadron—a very great pity."

On hearing this, all the men of *La Marie* turned towards Yann to learn if he already knew anything of the sad news.

"Ay," he answered in a low voice, but with an indifferent and haughty air, "it was told me in the last letter my father sent me." They still kept on looking at him, curious at finding out the secret of his grief, and it made him angry.

These questions and answers were rapidly exchanged through the pallid mists, so the moments of this peculiar colloquy skipped swiftly by.

"My wife wrote me at the same time," continued Larvoer, "that Monsieur Mevel's daughter has left the town to live at Ploubazlanec and take care of her old grand-aunt—Granny Moan. She goes out to needlework by the day now—to earn her living. Anyhow, I always thought, I did, that she was a good, brave girl, in spite of her fine-lady airs and her furbelows."

Then again they all stared at Yann, which made him still more angry; a red flush mounted to his cheeks, under their tawny tan.

With Larvoer's expression of opinion about Gaud ended this parley with the crew of the *Reine-Berthe*, none of whom were ever again to be seen by human eyes. For a moment their faces became more dim, their vessel being already farther away; and then, all at once, the men of the *Marie* found they had nothing to push against, nothing at the end of their poles—all spars, oars, odds and ends of deck-lumber, were groping and quivering in emptiness, till they fell heavily, one after the other, down into the sea, like their own arms, lopped off and inert.

They pulled all the useless defences on board. The *Reine-Berthe*, melting away into the thick fog, had disappeared as suddenly as a painted ship in a dissolving view. They tried to hail her, but the only response was a sort of mocking clamour—as of many voices—ending in a moan, that made them all stare at each other in surprise.

This *Reine-Berthe* did not come back with the other Icelandic fishers; and as the men of the *Samuel-Azenide* afterward picked up in some fjord an unmistakable waif (part of her taffrail with a bit of her keel), all ceased to hope; in the month of October the names of all her crew were inscribed upon black slabs in the church.

From the very time of that apparition—the date of which was well remembered by the men of the *Marie*—until the time of their return, there had been no really dangerous weather on the Icelandic seas, but a great storm from the west had, three weeks before, swept several sailors overboard, and swallowed up two vessels. The men remembered Larvoer's peculiar smile, and putting things together many strange conjectures were made. In the dead of night, Yann, more than once, dreamed that he again saw the sailor who blinked like an ape, and some of the men of the *Marie* wondered if, on that remembered morning, they had not been talking with ghosts.

CHAPTER XII—THE STRANGE COUPLE

Summer advanced, and, at the end of August, with the first autumnal mists, the Icelanders came home.

For the last three months the two lone women had lived together at Ploubazlanec in the Moan's cottage. Gaud filled a daughter's place in the poor birthplace of so many dead sailors. She had sent hither all that remained from the sale of her father's house; her grand bed in the town fashion, and her fine, different coloured dresses. She had made herself a plainer black dress, and like old Yvonne, wore a mourning cap, of thick white muslin, adorned merely with simple plaits. Every day she went out sewing at the houses of the rich people in the town, and returned every evening without being detained on her way home by any sweetheart. She had remained as proud as ever, and was still respected as a fine lady; and as the lads bade her good-night, they always raised a hand to their caps.

Through the sweet evening twilight, she walked home from Paimpol, all along the cliff road inhaling the fresh, comforting sea air. Constant sitting at needlework had not deformed her like many others, who are always bent in two over their work—and she drew up her beautiful supple form perfectly erect in looking over the sea, fairly across to where Yann was it seemed.

The same road led to his home. Had she walked on much farther, towards a well-known rocky windswept nook, she would come to that hamlet of Pors-Even, where the trees, covered with gray moss, grew crampedly between the stones, and are slanted over lowly by the western gales. Perhaps she might never more return there, although it was only a league away; but once in her lifetime she had been there, and that was enough to cast a charm over the whole road; and, besides, Yann would certainly often pass that way, and she could fancy seeing him upon the bare moor, stepping between the stumpy reeds.

She loved the whole region of Ploubazlanec, and was almost happy that fate had driven her there; she never could have become resigned to live in any other place.

Towards this end of August, a southern warmth, diffusing languor, rises and spreads towards the north, with luminous afterglows and stray rays from a distant sun, which float over the Breton seas. Often the air is calm and pellucid, without a single cloud on high.

At the hour of Gaud's return journey, all things had already begun to fade in the nightfall, and become fused into close, compact groups. Here and there a clump of reeds strove to make way between stones, like a battle-torn flag; in a hollow, a cluster of gnarled trees formed a dark mass, or else some straw-thatched hamlet indented the moor. At the cross-roads the images of Christ on the cross, which watch over and protect the country, stretched out their black arms on their supports like real men in torture; in the distance the Channel appeared fair and calm, one vast golden mirror, under the already darkened sky and shade-laden horizon.

In this country even the calm fine weather was a melancholy thing; notwithstanding, a vague uneasiness seemed to hover about; a palpable dread emanating from the sea to which so many lives are intrusted, and whose everlasting threat only slumbered.

Gaud sauntered along as in a dream, and never found the way long enough. The briny smell of the shore, and a sweet odour of flowerets growing along the cliffs amid thorny bushes, perfumed the air. Had it not been for Granny Yvonne waiting for her at home, she would have loitered along the reed-strewn paths, like the beautiful ladies in stories, who dream away the summer evenings in their fine parks.

Many thoughts of her early childhood came back to her as she passed through the country; but they seemed so effaced and far away now, eclipsed by her love looming up between.

In spite of all, she went on thinking of Yann as engaged in a degree—a restless, scornful betrothed, whom she never would really have, but to whom she persisted in being faithful in mind, without speaking about it to any one. For the time, she was happy to know that he was off Iceland; for there, at least, the sea would keep him lonely in her deep cloisters, and he would belong to no other woman.

True, he would return one of these days, but she looked upon that return more calmly than before. She instinctively understood that her poverty would not be a reason for him to despise her; for he was not as other men. Moreover, the death of poor Sylvestre would draw them closer together. Upon his return, he could not do otherwise than come to see his friend's old granny; and Gaud had decided to be present at that visit; for it did not seem to her that it would be undignified. Appearing to remember nothing, she would talk to him as to a long-known friend; she would even speak with affection, as was due to Sylvestre's brother, and try to seem easy and natural. And who knows? Perhaps it would not be impossible to be as a sister to him, now that she was so lonely in the world; to rely upon his friendship, even to ask it as a support, with enough preliminary explanation for him not to accuse her of any after-thought of marriage.

She judged him to be untamed and stubborn in his independent ideas, yet tender and loyal, and capable of understanding the goodness that comes straight from the heart.

How would he feel when he met her again, in her poor ruined home? Very, very poor she was—for Granny Moan was not strong enough now to go out washing, and only had her small widow's pension left; granted, she ate but little, and the two could still manage to live, not dependent upon others.

Night was always fallen when she arrived home; before she could enter she had to go down a little over the worn rocks, for the cottage was placed on an incline towards the beach, below the level of the Ploubazlanec roadside. It was almost hidden under its thick brown straw thatch, and looked like the back of some huge beast, shrunk down under its bristling fur. Its walls were sombre and rough like the rocks, but with tiny tufts of green moss and lichens over them. There were three uneven steps before the threshold, and the inside latch was opened by a length of rope-yarn run through a hole. Upon entering, the first thing to be seen was the window, hollowed out through the wall as in the substance of a rampart, and giving view of the sea, whence inflowed a dying yellow light. On the hearth burned brightly the sweet-scented branches of pine and beechwood that old Yvonne used to pick up along the way, and she herself was sitting there, seeing to their bit of supper; indoors she wore a kerchief over her head to save her cap. Her still beautiful profile was outlined in the red flame of her fire. She looked up at Gaud. Her eyes, which formerly were brown, had taken a faded look, and almost appeared blue; they seemed no longer to see, and were troubled and uncertain with old age. Each day she greeted Gaud with the same words:

"Oh, dear me! my good lass, how late you are to-night!"

"No, Granny," answered Gaud, who was used to it. "This is the same time as other days."

"Eh? It seemed to me, dear, later than usual."

They sat down to supper at their table, which had almost become shapeless from constant use, but was still as thick as the generous slice of a huge oak. The cricket began its silver-toned music again.

One of the sides of the cottage was filled up by roughly sculptured, worm-eaten woodwork, which had an opening wherein were set the sleeping bunks, where generations of fishers had been born, and where their aged mothers had died.

Quaint old kitchen utensils hung from the black beams, as well as bunches of sweet herbs, wooden spoons, and smoked bacon; fishing-nets, which had been left there since the shipwreck of the last Moans, their meshes nightly bitten by the rats.

Gaud's bed stood in an angle under its white muslin draperies; it seemed like a very fresh and elegant modern invention brought into the hut of a Celt.

On the granite wall hung a photograph of Sylvestre in his sailor clothes. His grandmother had fixed his military medal to it, with his own pair of those red cloth anchors that French men-of-wars-men wear on their right sleeve; Gaud had also brought one of those funereal crowns, of black and white beads, placed round the portraits of the dead in Brittany. This represented Sylvestre's mausoleum, and was all that remained to consecrate his memory in his own land.

On summer evenings they did not sit up late, to save the lights; when the weather was fine, they sat out a while on a stone bench before the door, and looked at passers-by in the road, a little over their heads. Then old Yvonne would lie down on her cupboard shelf; and Gaud on her fine bed, would fall asleep pretty soon, being tired out with her day's work, and walking, and dreaming of the return of the Icelanders. Like a wise, resolute girl, she was not too greatly apprehensive.

CHAPTER XIII—RENEWED DISAPPOINTMENT

But one day in Paimpol, hearing that *La Marie* had just got in, Gaud felt possessed with a kind of fever. All her quiet composure disappeared; she abruptly finished up her work, without quite knowing why, and set off home sooner than usual.

Upon the road, as she hurried on, she recognised *him*, at some distance off, coming towards her. She trembled and felt her strength giving way. He was now quite close, only about twenty steps off, his head erect and his hair curling out from beneath his fisher's cap. She was so taken by surprise at this meeting, that she was afraid she might fall, and then he would understand all; she would die of very shame at it. She thought, too, she was not looking well, but wearied by the hurried work. She would have done anything to be hidden away under the reeds or in one of the ferret-holes.

He also had taken a backward step, as if to turn in another direction. But it was too late now. Both met in the narrow path. Not to touch her, he drew up against the bank, with a side swerve like a skittish horse, looking at her in a wild, stealthy way.

She, too, for one half second looked up, and in spite of herself mutely implored him, with an agonized prayer. In that involuntary meeting of their eyes, swift as the firing of a gun, these gray pupils of hers had appeared to dilate and light up with some grand noble thought, which flashed forth in a blue flame, while the blood rushed crimson even to her temples beneath her golden tresses.

As he touched his cap he faltered. "Wish you good-day, Mademoiselle Gaud."

"Good-day, Monsieur Yann," she answered.

That was all. He passed on. She went on her way, still quivering, but feeling, as he disappeared, that her blood was slowly circulating again and her strength returning.

At home, she found Granny Moan crouching in a corner with her head held between her hands, sobbing with her childish "he, he!" her hair dishevelled and falling from beneath her cap like thin skeins of gray hemp.

"Oh, my kind Gaud! I've just met young Gaos down by Plouherzel as I came back from my wood-gathering; we spoke of our poor lad, of course. They arrived this morning from Iceland, and in the afternoon he came over to see me while I was out. Poor lad, he had tears in his eyes, too. He came right up to my door, my kind Gaud, to carry my little fagot."

She listened, standing, while her heart seemed almost to break; so this visit of Yann's, upon which she had so much relied for saying so many things, was already over, and would doubtless not occur again. It was all done. Her poor heart seemed more lonely than ever. Her misery harder, and the world more empty; and she hung her head with a wild desire to die.

CHAPTER XIV—THE GRANDAM BREAKING UP

Slowly the winter drew nigh, and spread over all like a shroud leisurely drawn. Gray days followed one another, but Yann appeared no more, and the two women lived on in their loneliness. With the cold, their daily existence became harder and more expensive.

Old Yvonne was difficult to tend, too; her poor mind was going. She got into fits of temper now, and spoke wicked, insulting speeches once or twice every week; it took her so, like a child, about mere nothings.

Poor old granny! She was still so sweet in her lucid days, that Gaud did not cease to respect and cherish her. To have always been so good and to end by being bad, and show towards the close a depth of malice and spitefulness that had slumbered during her whole life, to use a whole vocabulary of coarse words that she had hidden; what mockery of the soul! what a derisive mystery! She began to sing, too, which was still more painful to hear than her angry words, for she mixed everything up together—the *oremus* of a mass with refrains of loose songs heard in the harbour from wandering sailors. Sometimes she sang "*Les Fillettes de Paimpol*" (The Lasses of Paimpol), or, nodding her head and beating time with her foot, she would mutter:

"Mon mari vient de partir; Pour la peche d'Islande, mon mari vient de partir, Il m'a laissee sans le sou, Mais—trala, trala la lou, J'en gagne, j'en gagne."

(My husband went off sailing Upon the Iceland cruise, But never left me money, Not e'en a couple sous. But—ri too loo! ri tooral loo! I know what to do!)

She always stopped short, while her eyes opened wide with a lifeless expression, like those dying flames that suddenly flash out before fading away. She hung her head and remained speechless for a great length of time, her lower jaw dropping as in the dead.

One day she could remember nothing of her grandson. "Sylvestre? Sylvestre?" repeated she, wondering whom Gaud meant; "oh! my dear, d'ye see, I've so many of them, that now I can't remember their names!"

So saying she threw up her poor wrinkled hands, with a careless, almost contemptuous toss. But the next day she remembered him quite well; mentioning several things he had said or done, and that whole day long she wept.

Oh! those long winter evenings when there was not enough wood for their fire; to work in the bitter cold for one's daily bread, sewing hard to finish the clothes brought over from Paimpol.

Granny Yvonne, sitting by the hearth, remained quiet enough, her feet stuck in among the smouldering embers, and her hands clasped beneath her apron. But at the beginning of the evening, Gaud always had to talk to her to cheer her a little.

"Why don't ye speak to me, my good girl? In my time I've known many girls who had plenty to say for themselves. I don't think it 'ud seem so lonesome, if ye'd only talk a bit."

So Gaud would tell her chit-chat she had heard in town, or spoke of the people she had met on her way home, talking of things that were quite indifferent to her, as indeed all things were now; and stopping in the midst of her stories when she saw the poor old woman was falling asleep.

There seemed nothing lively or youthful around her, whose fresh youth yearned for youth. Her beauty would fade away, lonely and barren. The wind from the sea came in from all sides, blowing her lamp about, and the roar of the waves could be heard as in a ship. Listening, the ever-present sad memory of Yann came to her, the man whose dominion was these battling elements; through the long terrible nights, when all things were unbridled and howling in the outer darkness, she thought of him with agony.

Always alone as she was, with the sleeping old granny, she sometimes grew frightened and looked in all dark corners, thinking of the sailors, her ancestors, who had lived in these nooks, but perished in the sea on such nights as these. Their spirits might possibly return; and she did not feel assured against the visit of the dead by the presence of the poor old woman, who was almost as one of them herself.

Suddenly she shivered from head to foot, as she heard a thin, cracked voice, as if stifled under the earth, proceed from the chimney corner.

In a chirping tone, which chilled her very soul, the voice sang:

"Pour la peche d'Islande, mon mari vient de partir, Il m'a laissee sans le sou, Mais—trala, trala la lou!"

Then she was seized with that peculiar terror that one has of mad people.

The rain fell with an unceasing, fountain-like gush, and streamed down the walls outside. There were oozings of water from the old moss-grown roof, which continued dropping on the self-same spots with a monotonous sad splash. They even soaked through into the floor inside, which was of hardened earth studded with pebbles and shells.

Dampness was felt on all sides, wrapping them up in its chill masses; an uneven, buffeting dampness, misty and dark, and seeming to isolate the scattered huts of Ploubazlanec still more.

But the Sunday evenings were the saddest of all, because of the relative gaiety in other homes on that day, for there are joyful evenings even among those forgotten hamlets of the coast; here and there, from some closed-up hut, beaten about by the inky rains, ponderous songs issued. Within, tables were spread for drinkers; sailors sat before the smoking fire, the old ones drinking brandy and the young ones flirting with the girls; all more or less intoxicated and singing to deaden thought. Close to them, the great sea, their tomb on the morrow, sang also, filling the vacant night with its immense profound voice.

On some Sundays, parties of young fellows who came out of the taverns or back from Paimpol, passed along the road, near the door of the Moans; they were such as lived at the land's end of Pors-Even way. They passed very late, caring little for the cold and wet, accustomed as they were to frost and tempests. Gaud lent her ear to the medley of their songs and shouts—soon lost in the uproar of the squalls or the breakers—trying to distinguish Yann's voice, and then feeling strangely perplexed if she thought she had heard it.

It really was too unkind of Yann not to have returned to see them again, and to lead so gay a life so soon after the death of Sylvestre; all this was unlike him. No, she really could not understand him now, but in spite of all she could not forget him or believe him to be without heart.

The fact was that since his return he had been leading a most dissipated life indeed. Three or four times, on the Ploubazlanec road, she had seen him coming towards her, but she was always quick enough to shun him; and he, too, in those cases, took the opposite direction over the heath. As if by mutual understanding, now, they fled from each other.

CHAPTER XV—THE NEW SHIP

At Paimpol lives a large, stout woman named Madame Tressoleur. In one of the streets that lead to the harbour she keeps a tavern, well known to all the Icelanders, where captains and ship-owners come to engage their sailors, and choose the strongest among them, men and masters all drinking together.

At one time she had been beautiful, and was still jolly with the fishers; she has a mustache, is as broad built as a Dutchman, and as bold and ready of speech as a Levantine. There is a look of the daughter of the regiment about her, notwithstanding her ample nun-like muslin headgear; for all that, a religious halo of its sort floats around her, for the simple reason that she is a Breton born.

The names of all the sailors of the country are written in her head as in a register; she knows them all, good or bad, and knows exactly, too, what they earn and what they are worth.

One January day, Gaud, who had been called in to make a dress, sat down to work in a room behind the tap-room.

To go into the abode of our Madame Tressoleur, you enter by a broad, massive-pillared door, which recedes in the olden style under the first floor. When you go to open this door, there is always some obliging gust of wind from the street that pushes it in, and the new-comers make an abrupt entrance, as if carried in by a beach roller. The hall is adorned by gilt frames, containing pictures of ships and wrecks. In an angle a china statuette of the Virgin is placed on a bracket, between two bunches of artificial flowers.

These olden walls must have listened to many powerful songs of sailors, and witnessed many wild gay scenes, since the first far-off days of Paimpol—all through the lively times of the privateers, up to these of the present Icelanders, so very little different from their ancestors. Many lives of men have been angled for and hooked there, on the oaken tables, between two drunken bouts.

While she was sewing the dress, Gaud lent her ear to the conversation going on about Iceland, behind the partition, between Madame Tressoleur and two old sailors, drinking. They were discussing a new craft that was being rigged in the harbour. She never would be ready for the next season, so they said of this *Leopoldine*.

"Oh, yes, to be sure she will!" answered the hostess. "I tell 'ee the crew was all made up yesterday—the whole of 'em out of the old *Marie* of Guermeur's, that's to be sold for breaking up; five young fellows signed their engagement here before me, at this here table, and with my own pen —so ye see, I'm right! And fine fellows, too, I can tell 'ee; Laumec, Tugdual Caroff, Yvon Duff, young Keraez from Treguier, and long Yann Gaos from Pors-Even, who's worth any three on 'em!"

The *Leopoldine*! The half-heard name of the ship that was to carry Yann away became suddenly fixed in her brain, as if it had been hammered in to remain more ineffaceably there.

At night back again at Ploubazlanec, and finishing off her work by the light of her pitiful lamp, that name came back to her mind, and its very sound impressed her as a sad thing. The names of vessels, as of things, have a significance in themselves—almost a particular meaning of their own. The new and unusual word haunted her with an unnatural persistency, like some ghastly and clinging warning. She had expected to see Yann start off again on the *Marie*, which she knew so well and had formerly visited, and whose Virgin had so long protected its dangerous voyages; and the change to the *Leopoldine* increased her anguish.

But she told herself that that was not her concern, and nothing about him ought ever to affect her. After all, what could it matter to her whether he were here or there, on this ship or another, ashore or not? Would she feel less miserable with him back in Iceland, when the summer would return over the deserted cottages, and lonely anxious women—or when a new autumn came again, bringing home the fishers once more? All that was alike indifferent to her, equally without joy or hope. There was no link between them now, nothing ever to bring them together, for was he not forgetting even poor little Sylvestre? So, she had plainly to understand that this sole dream of her life was over for ever; she had to forget Yann, and all things appertaining to his existence, even the very name of Iceland, which still vibrated in her with so painful a charm—because of him all such thoughts must be swept away. All was indeed over, for ever and ever.

She tenderly looked over at the poor old woman asleep, who still required all her attention, but who would soon die. Then, what would be the good of living and working after that; of what use would she be?

Out of doors, the western wind had again risen; and, notwithstanding its deep distant soughing, the soft regular patter of the eaves-droppings could be heard as they dripped from the roof. And so the tears of the forsaken one began to flow—tears running even to her lips to impart their briny taste, and dropping silently on her work, like summer showers brought by no breeze, but suddenly falling, hurried and heavy, from the over-laden clouds; as she could no longer see to work, and she felt worked out and discouraged before this great hollowness of her life, she folded up the extra-sized body of Madame Tressoleur and went to bed.

She shivered upon that fine, grand bed, for, like all things in the cottage, it seemed also to be getting colder and damper. But as she was very young, although she still continued weeping, it ended by her growing warm and falling asleep.

CHAPTER XVI—LONE AND LORN

Other sad weeks followed on, till it was early February, fine, temperate weather. Yann had just come from his shipowner's where he had received his wages for the last summer's fishery, fifteen hundred francs, which, according to the custom of the family, he carried to his mother. The catch had been a good one, and he returned well pleased.

Nearing Ploubazlanec, he spied a crowd by the side of the road. An old woman was gesticulating with her stick, while the street boys mocked and laughed around her. It was Granny Moan. The good old granny whom Sylvestre had so tenderly loved—her dress torn and bedraggled—had now become one of those poor old women, almost fallen back in second childhood, who are followed and ridiculed along their roads. The sight hurt him cruelly.

The boys of Ploubazlanec had killed her cat, and she angrily and despairingly threatened them with her stick. "Ah, if my poor lad had only been here! for sure, you'd never dared do it, you young rascals!"

It appeared that as she ran after them to beat them, she had fallen down; her cap was awry, and her dress covered with mud; they called out that she was tipsy (as often happens to those poor old "grizzling" people in the country who have met misfortune).

But Yann clearly knew that that was not true, and that she was a very respectable old woman, who only drank water.

"Aren't you ashamed?" roared he to the boys.

He was very angry, and his voice and tone frightened them, so that in the twinkling of an eye they all took flight, frightened and confused before "Long Gaos."

Gaud, who was just returning from Paimpol, bringing home her work for the evening, had seen all this from afar, and had recognised Granny in the group. She eagerly rushed forward to learn what the matter was, and what they had done to her; seeing the cat, she understood it all. She lifted up her frank eyes to Yann, who did not look aside; neither thought of avoiding each other now; but they both blushed deeply and they gazed rather startled at being so near one another; but without hatred, almost with affection, united as they were in this common impulse of pity and protection.

The school-children had owed a grudge to the poor dead grimalkin for some time, because he had a black, satanic look; though he was really a very good cat, and when one looked closely at him, he was soft and caress-inviting of coat. They had stoned him to death, and one of his eyes hung out. The poor old woman went on grumbling, shaking with emotion, and carrying her dead cat by the tail, like a dead rabbit.

"Oh, dear, oh, dear! my poor boy, my poor lad, if he were only here; for sure, they'd never dared a-do it."

Tears were falling down in her poor wrinkles; and her rough blue-veined hands trembled.

Gaud had put her cap straight again, and tried to comfort her with soothing words. Yann was quite indignant to think that little children could be so cruel as to do such a thing to a poor aged woman and her pet. Tears almost came into his eyes, and his heart ached for the poor old dame as he thought of Sylvestre, who had loved her so dearly, and the terrible pain it would have been to him to see her thus, under derision and in misery.

Gaud excused herself as if she were responsible for her state. "She must have fallen down," she said in a low voice; "'tis true her dress isn't new, for we're not very rich, Monsieur Yann; but I mended it again only yesterday, and this morning when I left home I'm sure she was neat and tidy."

He looked at her steadfastly, more deeply touched by that simple excuse than by clever phrases or self-reproaches and tears. Side by side they walked on to the Moans' cottage. He always had acknowledged her to be lovelier than any other girl, but it seemed to him that she was even more beautiful now in her poverty and mourning. She wore a graver look, and her gray eyes had a more reserved expression, and nevertheless seemed to penetrate to the inner depth of the soul. Her figure, too, was thoroughly formed. She was twenty-three now, in the full bloom of her loveliness. She looked like a genuine fisher's daughter, too, in her plain black gown and cap; yet one could not precisely tell what gave her that unmistakable token of the lady; it was involuntary and concealed within herself, and she could not be blamed for it; only perhaps her bodice was a trifle nicer fitting than the others, though from sheer inborn taste, and showed to advantage her rounded bust and perfect arms. But, no! the mystery was revealed in her quiet voice and look.

CHAPTER XVII—THE ESPOUSAL

It was manifest that Yann meant to accompany them; perhaps all the way home. They walked on, all three together, as if following the cat's funeral procession; it was almost comical to watch them pass; and the old folks on the doorsteps grinned at the sight. Old Yvonne, in the middle, carried the dead pet; Gaud walked on her right, trembling and blushing, and tall Yann on the left, grave and haughty.

The aged woman had become quiet now; she had tidied her hair up herself and walked silently, looking alternately at them both from the tail of her eyes, which had become clear again.

Gaud said nothing for fear of giving Yann the opportunity of taking his leave; she would have liked to feel his kind, tender eyes eternally on her, and to walk along with her own closed so as to think of nothing else; to wander along thus by his side in the dream she was weaving, instead of arriving so soon at their lonely, dark cottage, where all must fade away.

At the door occurred one of those moments of indecision when the heart seems to stop beating. The grandam went in without turning round, then Gaud, hesitating, and Yann, behind, entered, too.

He was in their house for the first time in his life—probably without any reason. What could he want? As he passed over the threshold he touched his hat, and then his eyes fell and dwelt upon Sylvestre's portrait in its small black-beaded frame. He went slowly up to it, as to a tomb.

Gaud remained standing with her hands resting on the table. He looked around him; she watched him take a silent inspection of their poverty. Very poor looked this cottage of the two forsaken women. At least he might feel some pity for her, seeing her reduced to this misery inside its plain granite and whitewash. Only the fine white bed remained of all past splendour, and involuntarily Yann's eyes rested there.

He said nothing. Why did he not go? The old grandmother, although still so sharp in her lucid intervals, appeared not to notice him. How odd! So they remained over against one another, seeming respectively to question with a yearning desire. But the moments were flitting, and each second seemed to emphasize the silence between them. They gazed at one another more and more searchingly, as if in solemn expectation of some wonderful, exquisite event, which was too long in coming.

"Gaud," he began, in a low grave voice, "if you're still of a mind now _____."

What was he going to say? She felt instinctively that he had suddenly taken a mighty resolution—rapidly as he always did, but hardly dared word it.

"If you be still of a mind—d'ye see, the fish has sold well this year, and I've a little money ahead——"

"If she were still of a mind!" What was he asking of her? Had she heard aright? She felt almost crushed under the immensity of what she thought she premised.

All the while, old Yvonne, in her corner, pricked up her ears, feeling happiness approach.

"We could make a splice on it—a marriage, right off, Mademoiselle Gaud, if you are still of the same mind?"

He listened here for her answer, which did not come. What could stop her from pronouncing that "yes?" He looked astonished and frightened, she could see that. Her hands clutched the table edge. She had turned quite white and her eyes were misty; she was voiceless, and looked like some maid dying in her flower.

"Well, Gaud, why don't you answer?" said Granny Yvonne, who had risen and come towards them. "Don't you see, it rather surprises her, Monsieur Yann. You must excuse her. She'll think it over and answer you later on. Sit you down a bit, Monsieur Yann, and take a glass of cider with us."

It was not the surprise, but ecstasy that prevented Gaud from answering; no words at all came to her relief. So it really was true that he was good and kind-hearted. She knew him aright—the same true Yann, her own, such as she never had ceased to see him, notwithstanding his sternness and his rough refusal. For a long time he had disdained her, but now he accepted her, although she was poor. No doubt it had been his wish all through; he may have had a motive for so acting, which she would know hereafter; but, for the present, she had no intention of asking him his meaning, or of reproaching him for her two years of pining. Besides, all that was past, ay, and forgotten now; in one single moment everything seemed carried away before the delightful whirlwind that swept over her life!

Still speechless, she told him of her great love and adoration for him by her sweet brimming eyes alone; she looked deeply and steadily at him, while the copious shower of happy tears poured adown her roseate cheeks.

"Well done! and God bless you, my children," said Granny Moan. "It's thankful I be to Him, too, for I'm glad to have been let grow so old to see this happy thing afore I go."

Still there they remained, standing before one another with clasped hands, finding no words to utter; knowing of no word sweet enough, and no sentence worthy to break that exquisite silence.

"Why don't ye kiss one another, my children? Lor'! but they're dumb! Dear me, what strange grandchildren I have here! Pluck up, Gaud; say some'at to him, my dear. In my time lovers kissed when they plighted their troth."

Yann raised his hat, as if suddenly seized with a vast, heretofore unfelt reverence, before bending down to kiss Gaud. It seemed to him that this was the first kiss worthy of the name he ever had given in his life.

She kissed him also, pressing her fresh lips, unused to refinements of caresses, with her whole heart, to his sea-bronzed cheek.

Among the stones the cricket sang of happiness, being right for this time. And Sylvestre's pitiful insignificant portrait seemed to smile on them out of its black frame. All things, in fact, seemed suddenly to throb with life and with joy in the blighted cottage. The very silence apparently burst into exquisite music; and the pale winter twilight, creeping in at the narrow window, became a wonderful, unearthly glow.

"So we'll go to the wedding when the Icelanders return; eh, my dear children?"

Gaud hung her head. "Iceland," the "*Leopoldine*"—so it was all real! while she had already forgotten the existence of those terrible things that arose in their way.

"When the Icelanders return."

How long that anxious summer waiting would seem!

Yann drummed on the floor with his foot feverishly and rapidly. He seemed to be in a great hurry to be off and back, and was telling the days to know if, without losing time, they would be able to get married before his sailing. So many days to get the official papers filled and signed; so many for the banns: that would only bring them up to the twentieth or twenty-fifth of the month for the wedding, and if nothing rose in the way, they could have a whole honeymoon week together before he sailed.

"I'm going to start by telling my father," said he, with as much haste as if each moment of their lives were now numbered and precious.

PART IV — YANN'S FIRST WEDDING

CHAPTER I—THE COURTING BY THE SEA

All sweethearts like to sit on the bench at their cottage door, when night falls.

Yann and Gaud did that likewise. Every evening they sat out together before the Moans' cottage, on the old granite seat, and talked love.

Others have the spring-time, the soft shadow of the trees, balmy evenings, and flowering rosebushes; they had only the February twilight, which fell over the sea-beaten land, strewn with eel-grass and stones. There was no branch of verdure above their heads or around them; nothing but the immense sky, over which passed the slowly wandering mists. And their flowers were brown sea-weeds, drawn up from the beach by the fishers, as they dragged their nets along.

The winters are not very severe in this part of the country, being tempered by currents of the sea; but, notwithstanding that, the gloaming was often laden with invisible icy rain, which fell upon their shoulders as they sat together. But they remained there, feeling warm and happy. The bench, which was more than a hundred years old, did not seem in the least surprised at their love, having seen many other pairs in its time; it had listened to many soft words, which are always the same on the lips of the young, from generation to generation; and it had become used to seeing lovers sit upon it again, when they returned to it old and trembling; but in the broad day, this time, to warm themselves in the last sun they would see.

From time to time Granny Moan would put her head out at the door to have a look at them, and try to induce them to come in. "You'll catch cold, my good children," said she, "and then you'll fall ill—Lord knows, it really isn't sensible to remain out so late."

Cold! they cold? Were they conscious of anything else besides the bliss of being together.

The passers-by in the evening down their pathway, heard the soft murmur of two voices mingling with the voice of the sea, down below at the foot of the cliffs. It was a most harmonious music; Gaud's sweet, fresh voice alternated with Yann's, which had soft, caressing notes in the lower tones. Their profiles could be clearly distinguished on the granite wall against which they reclined; Gaud with her white headgear and slender black-robed figure, and beside her the broad, square shoulders of her beloved. Behind and above rose the ragged dome of the straw thatch, and the darkening, infinite, and colourless waste of the sea and sky floated over all.

Finally, they did go in to sit down by the hearth, whereupon old Yvonne immediately nodded off to sleep, and did not trouble the two lovers very much. So they went on communing in a low voice, having to make up for two years of silence; they had to hurry on their courtship because it was to last so short a time.

It was arranged that they were to live with Granny Moan, who would leave them the cottage in her will; for the present, they made no alterations in it, for want of time, and put off their plan for embellishing their poor lonely home until the fisherman's return from Iceland.

CHAPTER II—THE SEAMAN'S SECRET

One evening Yann amused himself by relating to his affianced a thousand things she had done, or which had happened to her since their first meeting; he even enumerated to her the different dresses she had had, and the jollifications to which she had been.

She listened in great surprise. How did he know all this? Who would have thought of a man ever paying any attention to such matters, and being capable of remembering so clearly?

But he only smiled at her in a mysterious way, and went on mentioning other facts to her that she had altogether forgotten.

She did not interrupt him; nay, she but let him continue, while an unexpected delicious joy welled up in her heart; she began, at length, to divine and understand everything. He, too, had loved—loved her, through that weary time. She had been his constant thought, as he was guilelessly confessing. But, in this case, what had been his reason for repelling her at first and making her suffer so long?

There always remained this mystery that he had promised to explain to her—yet still seemed to elude—with a confused, incomprehensible smile.

CHAPTER III—THE OMINOUS WEDDING-DRESS

One fine day, the loving pair went over to Paimpol, with Granny Moan, to buy the wedding-dress.

Gaud could very easily have done over one of her former town-lady's dresses for the occasion. But Yann had wanted to make her this present, and she had not resisted too long the having a dress given by her betrothed, and paid for by the money he had earned at his fishing; it seemed as if she were already his wife by this act.

They chose black, for Gaud had not yet left off mourning for her father; but Yann did not find any of the stuffs they placed before them good enough. He was not a little overbearing with the shopman; he, who formerly never would have set his foot inside a shop, wanted to manage everything himself, even to the very fashion of the dress. He wished it adorned with broad beads of velvet, so that it would be very fine, in his mind.

CHAPTER IV—FLOWER OF THE THORN

One evening as these lovers sat out on their stone bench in the solitude over which the night fell, they suddenly perceived a hawthorn bush, which grew solitarily between the rocks, by the side of the road, covered with tiny flowered tufts.

"It looks as if 'twas in bloom," said Yann.

They drew near to inspect it. It was in full flower, indeed. As they could not see very well in the twilight, they touched the tiny blooms, wet with mist. Then the first impression of spring came to them at the same time they noticed this; the days had already lengthened, the air was warmer, and the night more luminous. But how forward this particular bush was! They could not find another like it anywhere around, not one! It had blossomed, you see, expressly for them, for the celebration of their loving plight.

"Oh! let us gather some more," said Yann.

Groping in the dark, he cut a nosegay with the stout sailor's knife that he always wore in his belt, and paring off all the thorns, he placed it in Gaud's bosom.

"You look like a bride now," said he, stepping back to judge of the effect, notwithstanding the deepening dusk.

At their feet the calm sea rose and fell over the shingle with an intermittent swash, regular as the breathing of a sleeper; for it seemed indifferent or ever favourable to the love-making going on hard by.

In expectation of these evenings the days appeared long to them, and when they bade each other good-bye at ten o'clock, they felt a kind of discouragement, because it was all so soon over.

They had to hurry with the official documents for fear of not being ready in time, and of letting their happiness slip by until the autumn, or even uncertainty.

Their evening courtship in that mournful spot, lulled by the continual even wash of the sea, with that feverish impression of the flight of time, was almost gloomy and ominous. They were like no lovers; more serious and restless were they in their love than the common run.

Yet Yann never told her what mysterious thing had kept him away from her for these two lonely years; and after he returned home of a night, Gaud grew uneasy as before, although he loved her perfectly—this she knew. It is true that he had loved her all along, but not as now; love grew stronger in his heart and mind, like a tide rising and overbrimming. He never had known this kind of love before.

Sometimes on their stone seat he lay down, resting his head in Gaud's lap like a caressing child, till, suddenly remembering propriety, he would draw himself up erect. He would have liked to lie on the very ground at her feet, and remain there with his brow pressed to the hem of her garments. Excepting the brotherly kiss he gave her when he came and went, he did not dare to embrace her. He adored that invisible spirit in her, which appeared in the very sound of her pure, tranquil voice, the expression of her smile, and in her clear eye.

CHAPTER V—THE COST OF OBSTINACY

One rainy evening they were sitting side by side near the hearth, and Granny Moan was asleep opposite them. The fire flames, dancing over the branches on the hearth, projected their magnified shadows on the beams overhead.

They spoke to one another in that low voice of all lovers. But upon this particular evening their conversation was now and again broken by long troubled silence. He, in particular, said very little and lowered his head with a faint smile, avoiding Gaud's inquiring eyes. For she had been pressing him with questions all the evening concerning that mystery that he positively would not divulge; and this time he felt himself cornered. She was too quick for him, and had fully made up her mind to learn; no possible shifts could get him out of telling her now.

"Was it any bad tales told about me?" she asked.

He tried to answer "yes," and faltered: "Oh! there was always plenty of rubbish babbled in Paimpol and Ploubazlanec."

She asked what, but he could not answer her; so then she thought of something else. "Was it about my style of dress, Yann?"

Yes, of course, that had had something to do with it; at one time she had dressed too grandly to be the wife of a simple fisherman. But he was obliged to acknowledge that that was not all.

"Was it because at that time we passed for very rich people, and you were afraid of being refused?"

"Oh, no! not that." He said this with such simple confidence that Gaud was amused.

Then fell another silence, during which the moaning of the sea-winds was heard outside. Looking attentively at him, a fresh idea struck her, and her expression changed.

"If not anything of that sort, Yann, *what* was it?" demanded she, suddenly, looking at him fair in the eyes, with the irresistible questioning look of one who guesses the truth, and could dispense with confirmation.

He turned aside, laughing outright.

So at last she had, indeed, guessed aright; he never could give her a real reason, because there was none to give. He had simply "played the mule" (as Sylvestre had said long ago). But everybody had teased him so much about that Gaud, his parents, Sylvestre, his Iceland mates, and even Gaud herself. Hence he had stubbornly said "no," but knew well enough in the bottom of his heart that when nobody thought any more about the hollow mystery it would become "yes."

So it was on account of Yann's childishness that Gaud had been languishing, forsaken for two long years, and had longed to die.

At first Yann laughed, but now he looked at Gaud with kind eyes, questioning deeply. Would she forgive him? He felt such remorse for having made her suffer. Would she forgive him?

"It's my temper that does it, Gaud," said he. "At home with my folks, it's the same thing. Sometimes, when I'm stubborn, I remain a whole week angered against them, without speaking to anybody. Yet you know how I love them, and I always end by doing what they wish, like a boy. If you think that I was happy to live unmarried, you're mistaken. No, it couldn't have lasted anyway, Gaud, you may be sure."

Of course, she forgave him. As she felt the soft tears fall, she knew they were the outflow of her last pangs vanishing before Yann's confession. Besides, the present never would have been so happy without all her suffering; that being over, she was almost pleased at having gone through that time of trial.

Everything was finally cleared up between them, in a very unexpected though complete manner; there remained no clouds between their souls. He drew her towards him, and they remained some time with their cheeks pressed close, requiring no further explanations. So chaste was their embrace, that the old grandam suddenly awaking, they remained before her as they were without any confusion or embarrassment.

CHAPTER VI—THE BRIDAL

It was six days before the sailing for Iceland. Their wedding procession was returning from Ploubazlanec Church, driven before a furious wind, under a sombre, rain-laden sky.

They looked very handsome, nevertheless, as they walked along as in a dream, arm-in-arm, like king and queen leading a long cortege. Calm, reserved, and grave, they seemed to see nothing about them; as if they were above ordinary life and everybody else. The very wind seemed to respect them, while behind them their "train" was a jolly medley of laughing couples, tumbled and buffeted by the angry western gale.

Many people were present, overflowing with young life; others turning gray, but these still smiled as they thought of *their* wedding-day and younger years. Granny Yvonne was there and following, too, panting a little, but something like happy, hanging on the arm of an old uncle of Yann's, who was paying her old-fashioned compliments. She wore a grand new cap, bought for the occasion, and her tiny shawl, which had been dyed a third time, and black, because of Sylvestre.

The wind worried everybody; dresses and skirts, bonnets and *coiffes*, were similarly tossed about mercilessly.

At the church door, the newly married couple, pursuant to custom, had bought two nosegays of artificial flowers, to complete their bridal attire. Yann had fastened his on anyhow upon his broad chest, but he was one of those men whom anything becomes. As for Gaud, there was still something of the lady about the manner in which she had placed the rude flowers in her bodice, as of old very close fitting to her unrivalled form.

The violin player, who led the whole band, bewildered by the wind, played at random; his tunes were heard by fits and starts betwixt the noisy gusts, and rose as shrill as the screaming of a sea-gull. All Ploubazlanec had turned out to look at them. This marriage seemed to excite people's sympathy, and many had come from far around; at each turn of the road there were groups stationed to see them pass. Nearly all Yann's mates, the Icelanders of Paimpol, were there. They cheered the bride and bridegroom as they passed; Gaud returned their greeting, bowing slightly like a town lady, with serious grace; and all along the way she was greatly admired.

The darkest and most secluded hamlets around, even those in the woods, had been emptied of all their beggars, cripples, wastrels, poor, and idiots on crutches; these wretches scattered along the road, with accordions and hurdy-gurdies; they held out their hands and hats to receive the alms that Yann threw to them with his own noble look and Gaud with her beautiful queenly smile. Some of these poor waifs were very old and wore gray

122

locks on heads that had never held much; crouching in the hollows of the roadside, they were of the same colour as the earth from which they seemed to have sprung, but so unformed as soon to be returned without ever having had any human thoughts. Their wandering glances were as indecipherable as the mystery of their abortive and useless existences. Without comprehending, they looked at the merrymakers' line pass by. It went on beyond Pors-Even and the Gaoses' home. They meant to follow the ancient bridal tradition of Ploubazlanec and go to the chapel of La Trinite, which is situated at the very end of the Breton country.

At the foot of the outermost cliff, it rests on a threshold of low-lying rocks close to the water, and seems almost to belong to the sea already. A narrow goat's path leads down to it through masses of granite.

The wedding party spread over the incline of the forsaken cape head; and among the rocks and stones, happy words were lost in the roar of the wind and the surf.

It was useless to try and reach the chapel; in this boisterous weather the path was not safe, the sea came too close with its high rollers. Its white-crested spouts sprang up in the air, so as to break over everything in a ceaseless shower.

Yann, who had advanced the farthest with Gaud on his arm, was the first to retreat before the spray. Behind, his wedding party had remained strewn about the rocks, in a semicircle; it seemed as if he had come to present his wife to the sea, which received her with scowling, ill-boding aspect.

Turning round, he caught sight of the violinist perched on a gray rock, trying vainly to play his dance tunes between gusts of wind.

"Put up your music, my lad," said Yann; "old Neptune is playing us a livelier tune than yours."

A heavily beating shower, which had threatened since morning, began to fall. There was a mad rush then, accompanied by outcries and laughter, to climb up the bluff and take refuge at the Gaoses'.

CHAPTER VII—THE DISCORDANT NOTE

The wedding breakfast was given at Yann's parents', because Gaud's home was so poor. It took place upstairs in the great new room. Five-and-twenty guests sat down round the newly married pair—sisters and brothers, cousin Gaos the pilot, Guermeur, Keraez, Yvon Duff, all of the old *Marie's* crew, who were now the *Leopoldine's*; four very pretty bridesmaids, with their hair-plaits wound round their ears, like the empresses' in ancient Byzantium, and their modern white caps, shaped like sea-shells; and four best men, all broad-shouldered Icelanders, with large proud eyes.

Downstairs, of course, there was eating and cooking going on; the whole train of the wedding procession had gathered there in disorder; and the extra servants, hired from Paimpol, well-nigh lost their senses before the mighty lumbering up of the capacious hearth with pots and pans.

Yann's parents would have wished a richer wife for their son, naturally, but Gaud was known now as a good, courageous girl; and then, in spite of her lost fortune, she was the greatest beauty in the country, and it flattered them to see the couple so well matched.

The old father was inclined to be merry after the soup, and spoke of the bringing up of his fourteen little Gaoses; but they were all doing well, thanks to the ten thousand francs that had made them well off.

Neighbour Guermeur related the tricks he played in the navy, yarns about China, the West Indies, and Brazil, making the young ones who would be off some day, open their eyes in wonderment.

"There is a cry against the sea-service," said the old sailor, laughing, "but a man can have fine fun in it."

The weather did not clear up; on the contrary, the wind and rain raged through the gloomy night; and in spite of the care taken, some of the guests were fidgety about their smacks anchored in the harbour, and spoke of getting up to go and see if all was right. But here a more jovial sound than ever was heard from downstairs, where the younger members of the party were supping together; cheers of joy and peals of laughter ascended. The little cousins were beginning to feel exhilarated by the cider.

Boiled and roasted meats had been served up with poultry, different kinds of fish, omelets and pancakes.

The debate had turned upon fishery and smuggling, and the best means of fooling the coast-guardsmen, who, as we all know, are the sworn enemies of honest seafarers.

Upstairs, at the grand table, old circumnavigators went so far as to relate droll stories, in the vernacular.

But the wind was raging altogether too strong; for the windows shook with a terrible clatter, and the man telling the tale had hurriedly ended to go and see to his smack.

Then another went on: "When I was bo's'n's mate aboard of the *Zenobie*, a-lying at Aden, and a-doing the duty of a corporal of marines, by the same token, you ought to ha' seen the ostridge feather traders a-trying to scramble up over the side. [*Imitating the broken talk*] 'Bon-joo, cap'n! we're not thiefs—we're honest merchants'—Honest, my eye! with a sweep of the bucket, a purtending to draw some water up, I sent 'em all flying back an oar's length. 'Honest merchants, are ye,' says I, 'then send us up a bunch of honest feathers first—with a hard dollar or two in the core of it, d'ye see, and then I'll believe in your honesty!' Why, I could ha' made my fortun' out of them beggars, if I hadn't been born and brought up honest myself, and but a sucking-dove in wisdom, saying nothing of my having a sweetheart at Toulon in the millinery line, who could have used any quantity of feathers——"

Ha! here's one of Yann's little brothers, a future Iceland fisherman, with a fresh pink face and bright eyes, who is suddenly taken ill from having drunk too much cider. So little Laumec has to be carried off, which cuts short the story of the milliner and the feathers.

The wind wailed in the chimney like an evil spirit in torment; with fearful strength, it shook the whole house on its stone foundation.

"It strikes me the wind is stirred up, acos we're enjoying of ourselves," said the pilot cousin.

"No, it's the sea that's wrathy," corrected Yann, smiling at Gaud, "because I'd promised I'd be wedded to *her*."

A strange languor seemed to envelop them both; they spoke to one another in a low voice, apart, in the midst of the general gaiety. Yann, knowing thoroughly the effect of wine, did not drink at all. Now and then he turned dull too, thinking of Sylvestre. It was an understood thing that there was to be no dancing, on account of him and of Gaud's dead father.

It was the dessert now; the singing would soon begin. But first there were the prayers to say, for the dead of the family; this form is never omitted, at all wedding-feasts, and is a solemn duty. So when old Gaos rose and uncovered his white head, there was a dead silence around.

"This," said he, "is for Guillaume Gaos, my father." Making the sign of the cross, he began the Lord's prayer in Latin: "*Pater noster, qui es in coelis, sanctificetur nomen tumm*——"

The silence included all, even to the joyful little ones downstairs, and every voice was repeating in an undertone the same eternal words.

"This is for Yves and Jean Gaos, my two brothers, who were lost in the Sea of Iceland. This is for Pierre Gaos, my son, shipwrecked aboard the *Zelie*." When all the dead Gaoses had had their prayers, he turned towards grandmother Moan, saying, "This one is for Sylvestre Moan."

Yann wept as he recited another prayer.

"*Sed libera nos a malo. Amen!*"

Then the songs began; sea-songs learned in the navy, on the forecastle, where we all know there are rare good vocalists.

"*Un noble corps, pas moins que celui des Zouaves,*" etc.

A noble and a gallant lad The Zouave is, we know, But, capping him for bravery, The sailor stands, I trow. Hurrah, hurrah! long life to him, Whose glory never can grow dim!

This was sung by one of the bride's supporters, in a feeling tone that went to the soul; and the chorus was taken up by other fine, manly voices.

But the newly wedded pair seemed to listen as from a distance. When they looked at one another, their eyes shone with dulled brilliance, like that of transparently shaded lamps. They spoke in even a lower voice, and still held each other's hands. Gaud bent her head, too, gradually overcome by a vast, delightful terror, before her master.

The pilot cousin went around the table, serving out a wine of his own; he had brought it with much care, hugging and patting the bottle, which ought not to be shaken, he said. He told the story of it. One day out fishing they saw a cask a-floating; it was too big to haul on board, so they had stove in the head and filled all the pots and pans they had, with most of its contents. It was impossible to take all, so they had signalled to other pilots and fishers, and all the sails in sight had flocked round the flotsam.

"And I know more than one old sobersides who was gloriously topheavy when we got back to Pors-Even at night!" he chuckled liquorishly.

The wind still went on with its fearful din.

Downstairs the children were dancing in rings; except some of the youngest, sent to bed; but the others, who were romping about, led by little Fantec (Francis) and Laumec (Guillaume), wanted to go and play outside. Every minute they were opening the door and letting in furious gusts, which blew out the candles.

The pilot cousin went on with his story. Forty bottles had fallen to his lot, he said. He begged them all to say nothing about it, because of "*Monsieur le Commissaire de l'Inscription Maritime,*" who would surely make a fuss over the undeclared find.

"But, d'ye see," he went on, "it sarved the lubbers right to heave over such a vallyble cask or let it 'scape the lashings, for it's superior quality, with sartinly more jinywine grape-juice in it than in all the wine-merchants' cellars of Paimpol. Goodness knows whence it came—this here castaway liquor."

It was very strong and rich in colour, dashed with sea-water, and had the flavour of cod-pickle, but in spite of that, relishable; and several bottles were emptied.

Some heads began to spin; the Babel of voices became more confused, and the lads kissed the lasses less surreptitiously.

The songs joyously continued; but the winds would not moderate, and the seamen exchanged tokens of apprehension about the bad weather increasing.

The sinister clamour without was indeed worse than ever. It had become one continuous howl, deep and threatening, as if a thousand mad creatures were yelling with full throats and out-stretched necks.

One might imagine heavy sea-guns shooting out their deafening boom in the distance, but that was only the sea hammering the coast of Ploubazlanec on all points; undoubtedly it did not appear contented, and Gaud felt her heart shrink at this dismal music, which no one had ordered for their wedding-feast.

Towards midnight, during a calm, Yann, who had risen softly, beckoned his wife to come to speak with him.

It was to go home. She blushed, filled with shame, and confused at having left her seat so promptly. She said it would be impolite to go away directly and leave the others.

"Not a bit on it," replied Yann, "my father allows it; we may go," and away he carried her.

They hurried away stealthily. Outside they found themselves in the cold, the bitter wind, and the miserable, agitated night. They began to run hand-in-hand.

From the height of the cliff-path, one could imagine, without seeing it, the furious open sea, whence arose all this hubbub. They ran along, the wind cutting their faces, both bowed before the angry gusts, and obliged to put their hands over their mouths to cover their breathing, which the wind had completely taken away at first.

He held her up by the waist at the outset, to keep her dress from trailing on the ground, and her fine new shoes from being spoiled in the water, which streamed about their feet, and next he held her round the neck, too, and continued to run on still faster. He could hardly realize that he loved her so much! To think that she was now twenty-three and he nearly twenty-eight; that they might have been married two years ago, and as happy then as to-night!

At last they arrived at home, that poor lodging, with its damp flooring and moss-grown roof. They lit the candle, which the wind blew out twice.

Old grandam Moan, who had been taken home before the singing began, was there. She had been sleeping for the last two hours in her bunk, the flaps of which were shut. They drew near with respect and peeped through the fretwork of her press, to bid her good-night, if by chance she were not asleep. But they only perceived her still venerable face and closed eyes; she slept, or she feigned to do so, not to disturb them.

They felt they were alone then. Both trembled as they clasped hands. He bent forward to kiss her lips; but Gaud turned them aside, through ignorance of that kind of kiss; and as chastely as on the evening of their betrothal, she pressed hers to Yann's cheek, which was chilled, almost frozen, by the wind.

It was bitterly cold in their poor, low-roofed cottage. If Gaud had only remained rich, what happiness she would have felt in arranging a pretty room, not like this one on the bare ground! She was scarcely yet used to these rugged granite walls, and the rough look of all things around; but her Yann was there now, and by his presence everything was changed and transfigured. She saw only her husband. Their lips met now; no turning aside. Still standing with their arms intertwined tightly to draw themselves together, they remained dumb, in the perfect ecstasy of a never-ending kiss. Their fluttering breath commingled, and both quivered as if in a burning fever. They seemed without power to tear themselves apart, and knew nothing and desired nothing beyond that long kiss of consecrated love.

She drew herself away, suddenly agitated. "Nay, Yann! Granny Yvonne might see us," she faltered.

But he, with a smile, sought his wife's lips again and fastened his own upon them, like a thirsty man whose cup of fresh water had been taken from him.

The movement they had made broke the charm of delightful hesitation. Yann, who, at the first, was going to kneel to her as before a saint, felt himself fired again. He glanced stealthily towards the old oaken bunk, irritated at being so close to the old woman, and seeking some way not to be spied upon, but ever without breaking away from those exquisite lips.

He stretched forth his arm behind him, and with the back of his hand dashed out the light, as if the wind had done it. Then he snatched her up in his arms. Still holding her close, with his mouth continually pressed to hers, he seemed like a wild lion with his teeth embedded in his prey. For her part she gave herself up entirely, to that body and soul seizure that was imperious and without possible resistance, even though it remained soft as a great all-comprising embrace.

Around them, for their wedding hymn, the same invisible orchestra, played on——"Hoo-ooh-hoo!" At times the wind bellowed out in its deep noise, with a *tremolo* of rage; and again repeated its threats, as if with refined cruelty, in low sustained tones, flute-like as the hoot of an owl.

The broad, fathomless grave of all sailors lay nigh to them, restless and ravenous, drumming against the cliffs with its muffled boom.

One night or another Yann would have to be caught in that maw, and battle with it in the midst of the terror of ice as well. Both knew this plainly.

But what mattered that now to them on land, sheltered from the sea's futile fury. In their poor gloomy cottage, over which tempest rushed, they scorned all that was hostile, intoxicated and delightfully fortified against the whole by the eternal magic of love.

CHAPTER VIII—THE BLISSFUL WEEK

For six days they were husband and wife. In this time of leave-taking the preparations for the Iceland season occupied everybody. The women heaped up the salt for the pickle in the holds of the vessels; the men saw to the masts and rigging. Yann's mother and sisters worked from morning till night at the making of the sou'westers and oilskin waterproofs.

The weather was dull, and the sea, forefeeling the approach of the equinoctial gales, was restless and heaving.

Gaud went through these inexorable preparations with agony; counting the fleeting hours of the day, and looking forward to the night, when the work was over, and she would have her Yann to herself.

Would he leave her every year in this way?

She hoped to be able to keep him back, but she did not dare to speak to him about this wish as yet. He loved her passionately, too; he never had known anything like this affection before; it was such a fresh, trusting tenderness that the same caresses and fondlings always seemed as if novel and unknown heretofore; and their intoxication of love continued to increase, and never seemed—never was satiated.

What charmed and surprised her in her mate was his tenderness and boyishness. This the Yann in love, whom she had sometimes seen at Paimpol most contemptuous towards the girls. On the contrary, to her he always maintained that kindly courtesy that seemed natural to him, and she adored that beautiful smile that came to him whenever their eyes met. Among these simple folk there exists the feeling of absolute respect for the dignity of the wife; there is an ocean between her and the sweetheart. Gaud was essentially the wife. She was sorely troubled in her happiness, however, for it seemed something too unhoped for, as unstable as a joyful dream. Besides, would this love be lasting in Yann? She remembered sometimes his former flames, his fancies and different love adventures, and then she grew fearful. Would he always cherish that infinite tenderness and sweet respect for her?

Six days of a wedded life, for such a love as theirs, was nothing; only a fevered instalment taken from the married life term, which might be so long before them yet! They had scarcely had leisure to be together at all and understand that they really belonged to one another. All their plans of life together, of peaceful joy, and settling down, was forcedly put off till the fisherman's return.

No! at any price she would stop him from going to this dreadful Iceland another year! But how should she manage? And what could they do for a livelihood, being both so poor? Then again he so dearly loved the sea. But in spite of all, she would try and keep him home another season; she would use all her power, intelligence, and heart to do so. Was she to be the wife of an Icelander, to watch each spring-tide approach with sadness, and pass the whole summer in painful anxiety? no, now that she loved him, above everything that she could imagine, she felt seized with an immense terror at the thought of years to come thus robbed of the better part.

They had one spring day together—only one. It was the day before the sailing; all the stores had been shipped, and Yann remained the whole day with her. They strolled along, arm-in-arm, through the lanes, like sweethearts again, very close to one another, murmuring a thousand tender things. The good folk smiled, as they saw them pass, saying:

"It's Gaud, with long Yann from Pors-Even. They were married only t'other day!"

This last day was really spring. It was strange and wonderful to behold this universal serenity. Not a single cloud marred the lately flecked sky. The wind did not blow anywhere. The sea had become quite tranquil, and was of a pale, even blue tint. The sun shone with glaring white brilliancy, and the rough Breton land seemed bathed in its light, as in a rare, delicate ether; it seemed to brighten and revive even in the utmost distance. The air had a delicious, balmy scent, as of summer itself, and seemed as if it were always going to remain so, and never know any more gloomy, thunderous days. The capes and bays over which the changeful shadows of the clouds no longer passed, were outlined in strong steady lines in the sunlight, and appeared to rest also in the long-during calm. All this made their loving festival sweeter and longer drawn out. The early flowers already appeared: primroses, and frail, scentless violets grew along the hedgerows.

When Gaud asked: "How long then are you going to love me, Yann?"

He answered, surprisedly, looking at her full in the face with his frank eyes: "Why, for ever, Gaud."

That word, spoken so simply by his fierce lips, seemed to have its true sense of eternity.

She leaned on his arm. In the enchantment of her realized dream, she pressed close to him, always anxious, feeling that he was as flighty as a wild sea-bird. To-morrow he would take his soaring on the open sea. And it was too late now, she could do nothing to stop him.

From the cliff-paths where they wandered, they could see the whole of this sea-bound country; which seems almost treeless, strewn with low, stunted bush and boulders. Here and there fishers' huts were scattered over the rocks, their high battered thatches made green by the cropping up of new mosses; and in the extreme distance, the sea, like a boundless transparency, stretched out in a never-ending horizon, which seemed to encircle everything.

She enjoyed telling him about all the wonderful things she had seen in Paris, but he was very contemptuous, and was not interested.

"It's so far from the coast," said he, "and there is so much land between, that it must be unhealthy. So many houses and so many people, too, about! There must be lots of ills and ails in those big towns; no, I shouldn't like to live there, certain sure!"

She smiled, surprised to see this giant so simple a fellow.

Sometimes they came across hollows where trees grew and seemed to defy the winds. There was no view here, only dead leaves scattered beneath their feet and chilly dampness; the narrow way, bordered on both sides by green reeds, seemed very dismal under the shadow of the branches; hemmed in by the walls of some dark, lonely hamlet, rotting with old age, and slumbering in this hollow.

A crucifix arose inevitably before them, among the dead branches, with its colossal image of Our Saviour in weather-worn wood, its features wrung with His endless agony.

Then the pathway rose again, and they found themselves commanding the view of immense horizons—and breathed the bracing air of sea-heights once more.

He, to match her, spoke of Iceland, its pale, nightless summers and sun that never set. Gaud did not understand and asked him to explain.

"The sun goes all round," said he, waving his arm in the direction of the distant circle of the blue waters. "It always remains very low, because it has no strength to rise; at midnight, it drags a bit through the water, but soon gets up and begins its journey round again. Sometimes the moon appears too, at the other side of the sky; then they move together, and you can't very well tell one from t'other, for they are much alike in that queer country."

To see the sun at midnight! How very far off Iceland must be for such marvels to happen! And the fjords? Gaud had read that word several times written among the names of the dead in the chapel of the shipwrecked, and it seemed to portend some grisly thing.

"The fjords," said Yann, "they are not broad bays, like Paimpol, for instance; only they are surrounded by high mountains—so high that they seem endless, because of the clouds upon their tops. It's a sorry country, I can tell you, darling. Nothing but stones. The people of Iceland know of no such things as trees. In the middle of August, when our fishery is over, it's quite time to return, for the nights begin again then, and they lengthen out very quickly; the sun falls below the earth without being able to get up, and that night lasts all the winter through. Talking of night," he continued, "there's a little burying-ground on the coast in one of the fjords, for Paimpol men who have died during the season or went down at sea; it's consecrated earth, just like at Pors-Even, and the dead have wooden crosses just like ours here, with their names painted on them. The two Goazdious from Ploubazlanec lie there, and Guillaume Moan, Sylvestre's grandfather."

She could almost see the little churchyard at the foot of the solitary capes, under the pale rose-coloured light of those never-ending days, and she thought of those distant dead, under the ice and dark winding sheets of the long night-like winters.

"Do you fish the whole time?" she asked, "without ever stopping?"

"The whole time, though we somehow get on with work on deck, for the sea isn't always fine out there. Well! of course we're dead beat when the night comes, but it gives a man an appetite—bless you, dearest, we regularly gobble down our meals."

"Do you never feel sick of it?"

"Never," returned he, with an air of unshaken faith which pained her; "on deck, on the open sea, the time never seems long to a man—never!"

She hung her head, feeling sadder than ever, and more and more vanquished by her only enemy, the sea.

PART V — THE SECOND WEDDING

CHAPTER I—THE START

After the spring day they had enjoyed, the falling night brought back the impression of winter, and they returned to dine before their fire, which was flaming with new branches. It was their last meal together; but they had some hours yet, and were not saddened.

After dinner, they recovered the sweet impression of spring again, out on the Pors-Even road; for the air was calm, almost genial, and the twilight still lingered over the land.

They went to see the family—for Yann to bid good-bye—and returned early, as they wished to rise with break of day.

The next morning the quay of Paimpol was crowded with people. The departures for Iceland had begun the day before, and with each tide there was a fresh fleet off. On this particular morning, fifteen vessels were to start with the *Leopoldine*, and the wives or mothers of the sailors were all present at the getting under sail.

Gaud, who was now the wife of an Icelander, was much surprised to find herself among them all, and brought thither for the same fateful purpose. Her position seemed to have become so intensified within the last few days, that she had barely had time to realize things as they were; gliding irresistibly down an incline, she had arrived at this inexorable conclusion that she must bear up for the present, and do as the others did, who were accustomed to it.

She never before had been present at these farewells; hence all was new to her. Among these women was none like her, and she felt her difference and isolation. Her past life, as a lady, was still remembered, and caused her to be set aside as one apart.

The weather had remained fine on this parting-day; but out at sea a heavy swell came from the west, foretelling wind, and the sea, lying in wait for these new adventurers, burst its crests afar.

Around Gaud stood many good-looking wives like her, and touching, with their eyes big with tears; others were thoughtless and lively; these had no heart or were not in love. Old women, threatened nearly by death, wept as they clung to their sons; sweethearts kissed each other; half-maudlin sailors sang to cheer themselves up, while others went on board with gloomy looks as to their execution.

Many sad incidents could be marked; there were poor luckless fellows who had signed their contracts unconsciously, when in liquor in the grog-shop, and they had to be dragged on board by force; their own wives helping the gendarmes. Others, noted for their great strength, had been drugged in drink beforehand, and were carried like corpses on stretchers, and flung down in the forecastles.

Gaud was frightened by all this; what companions were these for her Yann? and what a fearful thing was this Iceland, to inspire men with such terror of it?

Yet there were sailors who smiled, and were happy; who, doubtless, like Yann, loved the untrammelled life and hard fishing work; those were the sound, able seamen, who had fine noble countenances; if they were unmarried they went off recklessly, merely casting a last look on the lasses; and if they were married, they kissed their wives and little ones, with fervent sadness and deep hopefulness as to returning home all the richer.

Gaud was a little comforted when she saw that all the *Leopoldines* were of the latter class, forming really a picked crew.

The vessels set off two by two, or four by four, drawn out by the tugs. As soon as they moved the sailors raised their caps and, full-voiced, struck up the hymn to the Virgin: "*Salut, Etoile-de-la-Mer!*" (All Hail! Star of the Sea!), while on the quay, the women waved their hands for a last farewell, and tears fell upon the lace strings of the caps.

As soon as the *Leopoldine* started, Gaud quickly set off towards the house of the Gaoses. After an hour and a half's walk along the coast, through the familiar paths of Ploubazlanec, she arrived there, at the very land's end, within the home of her new family.

The *Leopoldine* was to cast anchor off Pors-Even before starting definitely in the evening, so the married pair had made a last appointment here. Yann came to land in the yawl, and stayed another three hours with her to bid her good-bye on firm land. The weather was still beautiful and spring-like, and the sky serene.

They walked out on the high road arm-in-arm, and it reminded them of their walk the day before. They strolled on towards Paimpol without any apparent object in view, and soon came to their own house, as if unconsciously drawn there; they entered together for the last time. Grandam Moan was quite amazed at seeing them together again.

Yann left many injunctions with Gaud concerning several of his things in his wardrobe, especially about his fine wedding clothes; she was to take them out occasionally and air them in the sun, and so on. On board ship the sailors learn all these household-like matters; but Gaud was amused to hear it. Her husband might have been sure, though, that all his things would be kept and attended to, with loving care.

But all these matters were very secondary for them; they spoke of them only to have something to talk about, and to hide their real feelings. They went on speaking in low, soft tones, as if fearing to frighten away the moments that remained, and so make time flit by more swiftly still. Their conversation was as a thing that had inexorably to come to an end; and the most insignificant things that they said seemed, on this day, to become wondrous, mysterious, and important.

At the very last moment Yann caught up his wife in his arms, and without saying a word, they were enfolded in a long and silent embrace.

He embarked; the gray sails were unfurled and spread out to the light wind that rose from the west. He, whom she still could distinguish, waved his cap in a particular way agreed on between them. And with her figure outlined against the sea, she gazed for a long, long time upon her departing love.

That tiny, human-shaped speck, appearing black against the bluish gray of the waters, was still her husband, even though already it became vague and indefinable, lost in the distance, where persistent sight becomes baffled, and can see no longer.

As the *Leopoldine* faded out of vision, Gaud, as if drawn by a magnet, followed the pathway all along the cliffs till she had to stop, because the land came to an end; she sat down at the foot of a tall cross, which rises amidst the gorse and stones. As it was rather an elevated spot, the sea, as seen from there, appeared to be rimmed, as in a bowl, and the *Leopoldine*, now a mere point, appeared sailing up the incline of that immense circle. The water rose in great slow undulations, like the upheavals of a submarine combat going on somewhere beyond the horizon; but over the great space where Yann still was, all dwelt calm.

Gaud still gazed at the ship, trying to fix its image well in her brain, so that she might recognise it again from afar, when she returned to the same place to watch for its home-coming.

Great swells now rolled in from the west, one after another, without cessation, renewing their useless efforts, and ever breaking over the same rocks, foaming over the same places, to wash the same stones. The stifled fury of the sea appeared strange, considering the absolute calmness of the air and sky; it was as if the bed of the sea were too full and would overflow and swallow up the strand.

The *Leopoldine* had grown smaller and smaller, and was lost in the distance. Doubtless the under-tow carried her along, for she moved swiftly and yet the evening breezes were very faint. Now she was only a tiny, gray touch, and would soon reach the extreme horizon of all visible things, and enter those infinite regions, whence darkness was beginning to come.

Going on seven o'clock, night closed, and the boat had disappeared. Gaud returned home, feeling withal rather brave, notwithstanding the tears that uncontainably fell. What a difference it would have been, and what still greater pain, if he had gone away, as in the two preceding years, without even a good-bye! While now everything was softened and bettered between them. He was really her own Yann, and she knew herself to be so truly loved, notwithstanding this separation, that, as she returned home alone, she felt at least consoled by the thought of the delightful waiting for that "soon again!" to be realized to which they had pledged themselves for the autumn.

CHAPTER II—THE FIRST OF THE FLEET

The summer passed sadly, being hot and uneventful. She watched anxiously for the first yellowed leaves, and the first gathering of the swallows, and blooming of the chrysanthemums. She wrote to Yann several times by the boats bound for Rykawyk, and by the government cruisers, but one never can be sure of such letters reaching their destination.

Towards the end of July, she received a letter from him, however. He told her that his health was good, that the fishing season promised to be excellent, and that he already had 1500 fish for his share. From beginning to end, it was written in the simple conventional way of all these Icelanders' home letters. Men educated like Yann completely ignore how to write the thousand things they think, feel, or fancy. Being more cultivated than he, Gaud could understand this, and read between the lines that deep affection that was unexpressed. Several times in the four-paged letter, he called her by the title of "wife," as if happy in repeating the word. And the address above: "*A Madame Marguerite Gaos, maison Moan, en Ploubazlanec*"—she was "Madame Marguerite Gaos" since so short a time.

She worked hard during these summer months. The ladies of Paimpol had, at first, hardly believed in her talent as an amateur dressmaker, saying her hands were too fine-ladyish; but they soon perceived that she excelled in making dresses that were very nice-fitting, so she had become almost a famous dressmaker.

She spent all her earnings in embellishing their home against his return. The wardrobe and old-shelved beds were all done up afresh, waxed over, and bright new fastenings put on; she had put a pane of glass into their little window towards the sea, and hung up a pair of curtains; and she had bought a new counterpane for the winter, with new chairs and table.

She had kept the money untouched that her Yann had left her, carefully put by in a small Chinese box, to show him when he returned. During the summer evenings, by the fading light, she sat out before the cottage door with Granny Moan, whose head was much better in the warm weather, and knitted a fine new blue wool jersey for her Yann; round the collar and cuffs were wonderful open-work embroideries. Granny Yvonne had been a very clever knitter in her day, and now she taught all she knew to Gaud. The work took a great deal of wool; for it had to be a large jersey to fit Yann.

But soon, especially in the evenings, the shortening of the days could be perceived. Some plants, which had put forth all their blossoms in July, began to look yellow and dying, and the violet scabious by the wayside bloomed for the second time, smaller now, and longer-stalked; the last days of August drew nigh, and the first return-ship from Iceland hove in sight one evening at the cape of Pors-Even. The feast of the returners began.

Every one pressed in a crowd on the cliff to welcome it. Which one was it?

It was the *Samuel-Azenide*, always the first to return.

"Surely," said Yann's old father, "the *Leopoldine* won't be long now; I know how 'tis out yonder: when one of 'em begins to start homeward, the others can't hang back in any peace."

CHAPTER III—ALL BUT TWO

The Icelanders were all returning now. Two ships came in the second day, four the next, and twelve during the following week. And, all through the country, joy returned with them, and there was happiness for the wives and mothers; and junkets in the taverns where the beautiful barmaids of Paimpol served out drink to the fishers.

The *Leopoldine* was among the belated; there were yet another ten expected. They would not be long now, and allowing a week's delay so as not to be disappointed, Gaud waited in happy, passionate joy for Yann, keeping their home bright and tidy for his return. When everything was in good order there was nothing left for her to do, and besides she could think of nothing else but her husband in her impatience.

Three more ships appeared; then another five. There were only two lacking now.

"Come, come," they said to her cheerily, "this year the *Leopoldine* and the *Marie-Jeanne* will be the last, to pick up all the brooms fallen overboard from the other craft."

Gaud laughed also. She was more animated and beautiful than ever, in her great joy of expectancy.

CHAPTER IV—STILL AT SEA

But the days succeeded one another without result. She still dressed herself every day, and with a joyful look, went down to the harbour to gossip with the other wives. She said that this delay was but natural; was it not the same event every year? These were such safe boats, and had such capital sailors.

But when at home alone, at night, a nervous, anxious shiver of anguish would run through her whole frame.

Was it right to be frightened already? Was there even a single reason to be so? But she began to tremble at the mere idea of grounds for being afraid.

CHAPTER V—SHARING THE DREAD

The tenth of September came. How swiftly the days flew by!

One morning, a true autumn morning, with cold mist falling over the earth, in the rising sun, she sat under the porch of the chapel of the shipwrecked mariners, where the widows go to pray, with eyes fixed and glassy, throbbing temples tightened as by an iron hand.

These sad morning mists had begun two days before, and on this particular day Gaud had awakened with a still more bitter uneasiness, caused by the forecast of advancing winter. Why did this day, this hour, this very moment, seem to her more painful than the preceding? Often ships are delayed a fortnight, even a month, for that matter.

But surely there was something different about this particular morning, for she had come to-day for the first time to sit in the porch of this chapel and read the names of the dead sailors, perished in their prime.

"In memory of GAOS, YVON, Lost at sea Near the Norden-Fjord."

Like a great shudder, a gust of wind rose from the sea, and at the same time something fell like rain upon the roof above. It was only the dead leaves though; many were blown in at the porch; the old wind-tossed trees of the graveyard were losing their foliage in this rising gale, and winter was marching nearer.

"Lost at sea, Near the Norden-Fjord, In the storm of the 4th and 5th of August, 1880."

She read mechanically under the arch of the doorway; her eyes sought to pierce the distance over the sea. That morning it was untraceable under the gray mist, and a dragging drapery of clouds overhung the horizon like a mourning veil.

Another gust of wind, and other leaves danced in in whirls. A stronger gust still, as if the western storm that had strewn those dead over the sea, wished to deface the very inscriptions that remembered their names to the living.

Gaud looked with involuntary persistency at an empty space upon the wall that seemed to yawn expectant. By a terrible impression she was pursued, the thought of a fresh slab which might soon, perhaps, be placed there, with another name which she did not even dare to think of in such a spot.

She felt cold, and remained seated on the granite bench, her head reclining against the stone wall.

. . . "near the Norden-Fjord, In the storm of the 4th and 5th of August, At the age of 23 years, *Requiescat in pace!*"

Then Iceland loomed up before her, with its little cemetery lighted up from below the sea-line by the midnight sun. Suddenly in the same empty space on the wall, with horrifying clearness she saw the fresh slab she was thinking of; a clear white one, with a skull and cross-bones, and in a flash of foresight, a name—the worshipped name of "Yann Gaos!" Then she suddenly and fearfully drew herself up straight and stiff, with a hoarse, wild cry in her throat like a mad creature.

Outside the gray mist of the dawn fell over the land, and the dead leaves were again blown dancingly into the porch.

Steps on the footpath? Somebody was coming? She rose and quickly smoothed down her cap and composed her face. Nearer drew the steps. She assumed the air of one who might be there by chance; for, above all, she did not wish to appear yet, like the widow of a shipwrecked mariner.

It happened to be Fante Floury, the wife of the second mate of the *Leopoldine*. She understood immediately what Gaud was doing there; it was useless to dissemble with her. At first each woman stood speechless before the other. They were angry and almost hated each other for having met with a like sentiment of apprehension.

"All the men of Treguier and Saint Brieuc have been back this week," said Fante at last, in a pitiless, muffled, half-irritated voice.

She carried a blessed taper in her hand, to offer up a prayer. Gaud did not wish yet to resort to that extreme resource of despairing wives. Yet silently she entered the chapel behind Fante, and they knelt down together side by side, like two sisters.

To the "Star of the Sea" they offered ardent imploring prayers, with their whole soul in them. A sound of sobbing was alone heard, as their rapid tears swiftly fell upon the floor. They rose together, more confident and softened. Fante held up Gaud, who staggered, and taking her in her arms, kissed her.

Wiping their eyes, and smoothing their dishevelled hair, they brushed off the salt dust from the flagstones, soiling their gowns, and they went away in opposite directions, without another word.

CHAPTER VI—ALL BUT ONE

This end of September was like another summer, only a little less lively. The weather was so beautiful, that had it not been for the dead leaves that fell upon the roads, one might have thought that June had come back again. Husbands and sweethearts had all returned, and everywhere was the joy of a second spring-time of love.

At last, one day, one of the missing ships was signalled. Which one was it?

The groups of speechless and anxious women had rapidly formed on the cliff. Gaud, pale and trembling, was there, by the side of her Yann's father.

"I'm almost sure," said the old fisher, "I'm almost sure it's them! A red rail and a topsail that clews up—it's very like them anyhow. What do you make it, Gaud?

"No, it isn't," he went on, with sudden discouragement; "we've made a mistake again, the boom isn't the same, and ours has a jigger sail. Well, well, it isn't our boat this time, it's only the *Marie-Jeanne*. Never mind, my lass, surely they'll not be long now."

But day followed day, and night succeeded night, with uninterrupted serenity.

Gaud continued to dress every day like a poor crazed woman, always in fear of being taken for the widow of a shipwrecked sailor, feeling exasperated when others looked furtively and compassionately at her, and glancing aside so that she might not meet those glances that froze her very blood.

She had fallen into the habit of going in the early morning right to the end of the headland, on the high cliffs of Pors-Even, passing behind Yann's old home, so as not to be seen by his mother or little sisters. She went to the extreme point of the Ploubazlanec land, which is outlined in the shape of a reindeer's horn upon the gray waters of the channel, and sat there all day long at the foot of the lonely cross, which rises high above the immense waste of the ocean. There are many of these crosses hereabout; they are set up on the most advanced cliffs of the seabound land, as if to implore mercy and to calm that restless mysterious power that draws men away, never to give them back, and in preference retains the bravest and noblest.

Around this cross stretches the ever-green waste, strewn with short rushes. At this great height the sea air was very pure; it scarcely retained the briny odour of the weeds, but was perfumed with all the exquisite ripeness of September flowers.

Far away, all the bays and inlets of the coast were firmly outlined, rising one above another; the land of Brittany terminated in ragged edges, which spread out far into the tranquil surface.

Near at hand the reefs were numerous, but out beyond nothing broke its polished mirror, from which arose a soft, caressing ripple, light and intensified from the depths of its many bays. Its horizon seemed so calm, and its depths so soft! The great blue sepulchre of many Gaoses hid its inscrutable mystery, while the breezes, faint as human breath, wafted to and fro the perfume of the stunted gorse, which had bloomed again in the lastest autumn sun.

At regular hours the sea retreated, and great spaces were left uncovered everywhere, as if the Channel was slowly drying up; then with the same lazy slowness, the waters rose again, and continued their everlasting coming and going, without any heed of the dead.

At the foot of the cross, Gaud remained, surrounded by these tranquil mysteries, gazing ever before her, until the night fell and she could see no more.

CHAPTER VII—THE MOURNER'S VISION

September had passed. The sorrowing wife took scarcely any nourishment, and could no longer sleep. She remained at home now, crouching low with her hands between her knees, her head thrown back and resting against the wall behind. What was the good of getting up or going to bed now? When she was thoroughly exhausted she threw herself, dressed, upon her bed. Otherwise she remained in the same position, chilled and benumbed; in her quiescent state, only her teeth chattered with the cold; she had that continual impression of a band of iron round her brows; her cheeks looked wasted; her mouth was dry, with a feverish taste, and at times a painful hoarse cry rose from her throat, and was repeated in spasms, while her head beat backward against the granite wall. Or else she called Yann by his name in a low, tender voice, as if he were quiet close to her, whispering words of love to her.

Sometimes she occupied her brain with thoughts of quite insignificant things; for instance, she amused herself by watching the shadow of the china Virgin lengthen slowly over the high woodwork of the bed, as the sun went down. And then the agonized thoughts returned more horrible, and her wailing cry broke out again as she beat her head against the wall.

All the hours of the day passed, and all the hours of evening, and of night, and then the hours of the morning. When she reckoned the time he ought to have been back, she was seized with a still greater terror; she wished to forget all dates and the very names of the days.

Usually there is some information concerning the wrecks off Iceland; those who return have seen the tragedy from afar, or else have found some wreckage or bodies, or have an indication to guess the rest. But of the *Leopoldine* nothing had been seen, and nothing was known. The *Marie-Jeanne* men, the last to have seen her, on the 2d of August, said that she was to have gone on fishing farther towards the north, and, beyond that, the secret was unfathomable.

Waiting, always waiting, and knowing nothing! When would the time come when she need wait no longer? She did not even know that; and, now, she almost wished that it might be soon.

Oh! if he were dead; let them at least have pity enough to tell her so! Oh! to see her darling, as he was at this very moment, that is, what was left him! If only the much-implored Virgin, or some other power, would do her the blessing to show her, by second-sight, her beloved! either living and working hard to return a rich man, or else as a corpse, surrendered by the sea, so that she might at least know a certainty.

Sometimes she was seized with the thought of a ship appearing suddenly upon the horizon; the *Leopoldine* hastening home. Then she would suddenly make an irreflected movement to rise, and rush to look out at the ocean, to see whether it were true.

But she would fall back. Alas! where was this *Leopoldine* now? Where could she be? Out afar, at that awful distance of Iceland, forsaken, crushed, and lost.

All ended by a never-fading vision appearing to her—an empty, sea-tossed wreck, slowly and gently rocked by the silent gray and rose-streaked sea; almost with soft mockery, in the midst of the vast calm of deadened waters.

CHAPTER VIII—THE FALSE ALARM

Two o'clock in the morning.

It was at night, especially, that she kept attentive to approaching footsteps; at the slightest rumour or unaccustomed noise her temples vibrated; by dint of being strained to outward things, they had become fearfully sensitive.

Two o'clock in the morning. On this night as on others, with her hands clasped and her eyes wide open in the dark, she listened to the wind, sweeping in never-ending tumult over the heath.

Suddenly a man's footsteps hurried along the path! At this hour who would pass now? She drew herself up, stirred to the very soul, her heart ceasing to beat.

Some one stopped before the door, and came up the small stone steps.

He!—O God!—he! Some one had knocked—it could be no other than he! She was up now, barefooted; she, so feeble for the last few days, had sprung up as nimbly as a kitten, with her arms outstretched to wind round her darling. Of course the *Leopoldine* had arrived at night, and anchored in Pors-Even Bay, and he had rushed home; she arranged all this in her mind with the swiftness of lightning. She tore the flesh off her fingers in her excitement to draw the bolt, which had stuck.

"Eh?"

She slowly moved backward, as if crushed, her head falling on her bosom. Her beautiful insane dream was over. She just could grasp that it was not her husband, her Yann, and that nothing of him, substantial or spiritual, had passed through the air; she felt plunged again into her deep abyss, to the lowest depths of her terrible despair.

Poor Fantec, for it was he, stammered many excuses, his wife was very ill, and their child was stifling in its cot, suddenly attacked with a malignant sore throat; so he had run over to beg for assistance on the road to fetch the doctor from Paimpol.

What did all this matter to her? She had gone mad in her own distress, and could give no thoughts to the troubles of others. Huddled on a bench, she remained before him with fixed, glazed eyes, like a dead woman's; without listening to him or even answering at random or looking at him. What to her was the speech the man was making?

He understood it all; and guessed why the door had been opened so quickly to him, and feeling pity for the pain he had unwittingly caused, he stammered out an excuse.

"Just so; he never had ought to have disturbed her—her in particular."

"I!" ejaculated Gaud, quickly, "why should I not be disturbed particularly, Fantec?"

Life had suddenly come back to her; for she did not wish to appear in despair before others. Besides, she pitied him now; she dressed to accompany him, and found the strength to go and see to his little child.

At four o'clock in the morning, when she returned to throw herself on the bed, sleep subdued her, for she was tired out. But that moment of excessive joy had left an impression on her mind, which, in spite of all, was permanent; she awoke soon with a shudder, rising a little and partially recollecting—she knew not what. News had come to her concerning her Yann. In the midst of her confusion of ideas, she sought rapidly in her mind what it could be, but there was nothing save Fantec's interruption.

For the second time she fell back into her terrible abyss, nothing changed in her morbid, hopeless waiting.

Yet in that short, hopeful moment she had felt him so near to her, that it was as if his spirit had floated over the sea unto her, what is called a foretoken (*pressigne*) in Breton land; and she listened still more attentively to the steps outside, trusting that some one might come to her to speak of him.

Just as the day broke Yann's father entered. He took off his cap, and pushed back his splendid white locks, which were in curls like Yann's, and sat down by Gaud's bedside.

His heart ached fully, too, for Yann, his tall, handsome Yann, was his first-born, his favourite and his pride; but he did not despair yet. He comforted Gaud in his own blunt, affectionate way; to begin with, those who had last returned from Iceland spoke of the increasing dense fogs that might well have delayed the vessel; and then, too, an idea struck him; they might possibly have stopped at the distant Faroe Islands on their homeward course, whence letters were so long in travelling. This had happened to him once forty years ago, and his own poor dead and gone mother had had a mass said for his soul. The *Leopoldine* was such a good boat, next to new, and her crew were such able-bodied seamen.

Granny Moan stood by them shaking her head; the distress of her granddaughter had almost given her back her own strength and reason; she tidied up the place, glancing from time to time at the faded portrait of Sylvestre, which hung upon the granite wall with its anchor emblems and mourning-wreath of black bead-work. Ever since the sea had robbed her of her own last offspring she believed no longer in safe returns; she only prayed through fear, bearing Heaven a grudge in the bottom of her heart.

But Gaud listened eagerly to these consoling reasonings; her large sunken eyes looked with deep tenderness out upon this old sire, who so much resembled her beloved one; merely to have him near her was like a hostage against death having taken the younger Gaos; and she felt reassured, nearer to her Yann. Her tears fell softly and silently, and she repeated again her passionate prayers to the "Star of the Sea."

149

A delay out at those islands to repair damages was a very likely event. She rose and brushed her hair, and then dressed as if she might fairly expect him. All then was not lost, if a seaman, his own father, did not yet despair. And for a few days, she resumed looking out for him again.

Autumn at last arrived, a late autumn too, its gloomy evenings making all things appear dark in the old cottage, and all the land looked sombre, too.

The very daylight seemed crepuscular; immeasurable clouds, passing slowly overhead, darkened the whole country at broad noon. The wind blew constantly with the sound of a great cathedral organ at a distance, but playing profane, despairing dirges; at other times the noise came close to the door, like the howling of wild beasts.

She had grown pale, aye, blanched, and bent more than ever, as if old age had already touched her with its featherless wing. Often did she finger the wedding clothes of her Yann, folding and unfolding them again and again like some maniac, especially one of his blue woolen jerseys, which still had preserved his shape; when she threw it gently on the table, it fell with the shoulders and chest well defined; so she placed it by itself on a shelf of their wardrobe, and left it there, so that it might for ever rest unaltered.

Every night the cold mists sank upon the land, as she gazed over the depressing heath through her little window, and watched the paltry puffs of white smoke arise from the chimneys of other cottages scattered here and there on all sides. There the husbands had returned, like wandering birds driven home by the frost. Before their blazing hearths the evenings passed, cosy and warm; for the spring-time of love had begun again in this land of North Sea fishermen.

Still clinging to the thought of those islands where he might perhaps have lingered, she was buoyed up by a kind hope and expected him home any day.

CHAPTER IX—WEDDED TO THE SEA

But he never returned. One August night, out off gloomy Iceland, mingled with the furious clamour of the sea, his wedding with the sea was performed. It had been his nurse; it had rocked him in his babyhood, and had afterward made him big and strong; then, in his superb manhood, it had taken him back again for itself alone. Profoundest mystery had surrounded this unhallowed union. While it went on, dark curtains hung pall-like over it as if to conceal the ceremony, and the ghoul howled in an awful deafening voice to stifle his cries. He, thinking of Gaud, his sole, darling wife, had battled with giant strength against this deathly rival, until he at last surrendered, with a deep death-cry like the roar of a dying bull, through a mouth already filled with water; and his arms were stretched apart and stiffened for ever.

All those he had invited in days of old were present at his wedding. All except Sylvestre, who had gone to sleep in the enchanted gardens far, far away, at the other side of the earth.

22962640R00087

Printed in Poland
by Amazon Fulfillment
Poland Sp. z o.o., Wrocław